EXPERT GIVER

NO STRINGS ATTACHED

JASON CAZES

Expert Giver LLC

Paperback ISBN: 978-0-578-21178-7
Hardback ISBN: 978-0-578-21179-4

Library of Congress Control Number: 2018913559

Cover Photo © 2020 Jason Cazes. All rights reserved - used with permission.

PRINTED IN THE UNITED STATES OF AMERICA

Table of Contents

List of Figures

List of Tables

There's a principle which is a bar against all information, which is proof against all arguments, and which cannot fail to keep a man in everlasting ignorance. That principle is contempt prior to investigation.

—Herbert Spencer

Introduction

In January of 2018, I had a series of four revelations. The content of the revelations was clarification on what we need to understand in order to evolve, what our purpose is here, and four goals for the world that were shown to me as follows: (1) a plan to provide clean drinking water to those without it; (2) a program to "adopt" the homeless (we do it for animals but not homeless, damaged, or rejected people); (3) the elimination of nuclear weapons with a one-minute per day commitment upon awakening in the morning; and (4) the creation of Expert Giver Groups.

I explain why and how our instinctual drives for sex and financial security, although necessary for survival, dominate our lives, causing selfish choices that justify neglecting and harming ourselves and others, keeping us depressed, restless, and discontented.

"The Golden Rule" applies here—meaning, *Do unto others as you wish to be done to yourself.* Why follow the Golden Rule? Because you reap what you sow, and what you give is what you get. Most people are in denial of this truth. Our selfish instincts lie to us. I was given clarity surrounding these truths, which I do my best to explain in this book.

Chapter 1:
Revelations

Before my revelations in January 2018, I had no solid concept of God, and had given up on trying to figure it out. My spiritual experience was more profound than I have ever heard of another human being having. I was shown truth of the greater reality with complete clarity through a series of revelations.

I ask that you keep an open mind. Some words, like *God*, have lots of baggage attached. I am giving my best attempt to describe many things that are not easy to explain with words.

I use several words and phrases interchangeably to describe the same thing; such as *God*, the *One Great Spirit*, the *Great Spirit of One*, the *One*, *Spirit*, and the *Holy Spirit*.

Revelation defined:
- *A surprising and previously unknown fact, especially one that is made known in a dramatic way.*
- *The divine or supernatural disclosure to humans of something relating to human existence or the world.*

We hear stories about people dying and coming back, who say they saw a white light at the end of a tunnel. I went to the end of that tunnel and came out on the other side. There, I was shown a four-part series of revelations. That happened to me in the first week of January 2018. I had an experience in the near-death realm. It was a spiritual journey beyond my ego self.

Do you really want the truth? Are you ready for the accountability and responsibility that come with knowing more? The truth isn't always what you want it to be. Our selfish, instinctual side will not want to acknowledge some of the truth. But the deeper part of us beyond our selfish instinctual drives loves the truth and wants it to be expressed through our choices here and now.

I met God.

In the spirit realm, beyond human consciousness, I was given a presentation that happened over a series of four "scenes" that I was shown in sequence, which ended in a "download" of information.

Below, I describe the messages that were given to me with each revelation, in the order they were shown. Each revelation, as it occurred, gave more meaning to the previous one, like pieces of a puzzle coming together to form a full picture.

Revelation 1: I Am

In my first revelation, I was in outer space inside a small, clear bubble-shaped enclosure. I was hugging someone, just floating in space locked in a full embrace, with the limitless universe of black space expanding out in every direction outside the enclosure. I slowly relaxed the embrace and pulled away to see whom I was hugging, and I discovered that I was looking at an identical twin of myself. I had been hugging myself. That was the first scene in the first revelation.

What I am about to explain will not make complete sense until the meanings of all the revelations are combined together. Also, the complete message and meaning of my revelations are further broken down and explained in more detail later in the book.

So, what was this first message showing me? To initially explain in vague terms, I was shown that I am God, and God is me. And not just "me" as in Jason, as if I were special apart from everyone else. No, God is you, too. God is me, you, and all of life.

Revelation 2: The One Became the Many

In my second revelation, the scene was again in outer space, with unlimited blackness expanding in all directions, except that there was a small lit-up room off in the distance. I could see that the room was about the size of a bedroom closet, with its light on. I could also see that, inside the room, there was a small young boy on the floor, playing with some toys. Initially, I couldn't see his face because he was turned away from me. I could see the back of his head, which was full of curly brown hair, while he pushed one of the toys around on the floor. He was kneeling as a child does, using his hands to play, when suddenly I became aware that I was looking at God.

In the next moment, I felt a sudden sense of overwhelming sadness for God, the boy, because he looked so lonely playing in that room all by himself in the middle of space, with no one else. I felt so sorry for him. He was by himself with nothing but a few toys to play with—forever. It seemed so limiting and confining. Then, as I was having those thoughts and feelings about him being so lonely, he turned his head around and looked up at me with the most beautiful beaming eyes and smile I had ever seen.

I understood instantly what he wanted to tell me when he

3

looked at me, without any words spoken. The message was, "I'm not alone—I made you, and everything else, to play with—forever. I am not limited or bound as one being. I divided myself up into separate parts and pieces."

Just as human children are part of their parents, we are all part of God. We are small, divided pieces of God, but mostly ignorant of that fact. We were designed and created to purposefully forget, so that we are given the ultimate gift: the gift of life, choice, free will, and individual creation here as humans. What an amazing gift God gave us—which, in a larger sense, the spiritual part of ourselves gave us.

God separated into many pieces in order to experience more. I cannot experience love without another, without you—meaning that "someone else" must be there for me to experience loving another. Imagine yourself in a box, in space, alone forever—not a pleasant thought. Lonely. Singular. Boring. Terrifying.

What we all want is to be loved—right? Love doesn't happen in isolation. It takes two to tango. When God began, in a state of One, God was a singular experience—just to be as One with itself. That is limited. But with God being unlimited, from the very start creative life began, continues to evolve, and will always occur infinitely and creatively as it wills. We humans are part of the examples that God made things more entertaining for itself. In a way, we are God's toys, playing with itself. Given the gift of free will and choice, we are expressions of life, of God.

All of life started from one singular presence. Then, being intelligent, all-powerful, and infinite, that Great Spirit of One divided itself up into different parts that appeared as individuals. We cannot fully understand this while we are in the human condition, with our limited self-awareness, operating from the logical perspective of a "separate" experience as an ego. This illusion of "being separate" is reinforced throughout human life, with memories building a self and an ego from the time of birth. Ultimately, we are shaping and part of One greater spirit behind the scenes. We are spiritually One, but appear as many.

Revelation 3: Everything Is Yours, Not Just Some of It

In the third revelation, I was shown an endless field of treasures that stretched into a distant horizon. The treasures were symbols of riches that I could relate to from both a human and a spiritual perspective. In the center of the field, there were two enormous coin-shaped objects that were spinning slowly in sync. One appeared to be platinum and the other gold. Both had what appeared to be Roman or Egyptian symbols embossed on them. Under the giant coins, which were hovering together, there was an endless field of treasures beyond human imagination. The revelation I was being shown was that everything belongs to me outside of this human experience. The revelation was symbolic in order to relate the magnitude of its meaning to my human perspective; that is, it relayed a message that made sense to a human perspective of consciousness.

This third revelation, combined with the first two, totally unlocked my complete awareness of just who and what I truly am. The visual representation was a reminder to me that everything is mine. The revelation was saying, "Look, everything in the entire universe is yours—not just some of it, *all* of it." I was reminded in that moment of who I am and what really *is* beyond this human experience—which is the greater spiritual part of what we are. To have been shown and reminded of that was so special—or rather, special multiplied by a trillion. When I came back to human consciousness from this revelation, all I could say was, "Thank you for showing me this, reminding me of who and what I really am. Thank you."

The good news for you is that we are all in this together, and it's all yours, too! All of us inherit all of it. It's all ours. Everything. Forever. The revelations were truly remarkable and amazing beyond words or description. They go so far beyond winning a lottery. Winning a lottery on Earth is only part of the riches here. I was reminded of what I already knew deep down, but had totally forgotten. It is a bliss that goes beyond description with language. To even get close to describing the feeling surrounding this experience would be to say that it was like the supercharged excitement and joy of a five-year-old kid waking up on Christmas morning and running into the living room to see what presents are under the tree. But multiply that feeling by at least a trillion.

As humans, we have the illusion that we are separate beings, disconnected from and not part of the same being, because that's what our senses tell us. We appear to be individuals. But behind the scenes, we are all One spiritually—altogether, and not separate. It is the ultimate puzzle here for us to discover. Realization of this truth is a true spiritual awakening.

Revelation 4: The Download

The fourth and final revelation in this series concluded with a huge "download" of information, instructions, and clarity—all in a single moment. This revelation, like the others, began in a scene in space where black darkness expanded out in all directions. Somewhere from off to my right in the distance, a long, enormous, matte-black, perfectly shaped rectangular object was slowly coming into my view. When it finally arrived before me, it stopped moving, as if it were in a presentation position. I saw that it had shiny, ancient-looking symbols all over it, as the coins did in my earlier revelation. Again, the symbols looked like a blend of Egyptian hieroglyphics and Roman elements. The object was incredibly beautiful and detailed. I didn't understand the symbols, but they were familiar to me in some way that I cannot explain. After a few moments, during which I studied the object and its details, there was a sudden burst and blast of information given to me all at once as a massive download from the object.

Then the scene immediately changed. The rectangular object was now gone, and I was instead viewing the Earth from some distant point in space where it appeared to be about the size of a basketball. While viewing my planet, I had razor-sharp clarity about the messages and goals I was given to deliver there.

After I received the four revelations, I spent every day during the next three and a half months audio-recording the messages I was to deliver by writing this book. It took that long to get all the information out, for it was a big download, which contained goals for the world and clarity about truthful religious messages that have been misinterpreted. The download gave me clarity on how we are really all One, revealing why the Golden Rule needs to be practiced: because what you give is what you get, and there is no escaping it, since ultimately I am you. So, helping me is helping you, which also means that hurting you is hurting me.

In addition, I was given ideas about a method and format that we can use to connect with each other regularly in person: the concept of no-cost, self-supporting Expert Giver Groups. These groups will be vehicles for us to connect with and support each other, with the purposes of managing our instinctual motives and obtaining and maintaining a spiritual awakening through accountability and service to others.

After the revelations, I was hyperaware of human limitations. Human consciousness is limited, with only so many words in our vocabulary, a limited range and number of feelings, a measurable up and down and left and right in a three-dimensional reality, and five senses that define our human consciousness reality and experience. We humans are working with a limited set of rules and understandings of what defines reality. I was shown a much greater reality that is not limited to a five-sense experience. The greater reality unlimited by human senses is impossible to completely describe with our vocabulary, but I can say that it involves unlimited potential and creation. It's all good—in fact, even better than you can imagine.

Human life on Earth is playing out as one big movie. It is our movie. We like movies with stories that depict battles between good and evil, that get tense near the end, and then conclude happily. The message I received in my download was intended to help us choose a better ending to our movie here.

Chapter 2:
Beliefs

Our Beliefs Create Our Reality

Belief defined:
- *A state or habit of mind in which trust or confidence is placed in some person or thing.*
- *Something that is accepted, considered to be true, or held as an opinion.*
- *Confidence in the truth or existence of something not immediately susceptible to rigorous proof.*
- *An opinion or conviction.*

All of us have beliefs that develop from our experiences, from what we have been told, from what we have read, and from adopting the beliefs of others. Our beliefs are set, and we are constantly defending them, even when they no longer serve us. As we grow older, it becomes hard to entertain new beliefs, let alone actually adopt them. We are like, "Nah, I've seen it all. I've heard it all before. I know what's what."

Are you open-minded to new ideas and new beliefs? Are you teachable? That requires humility. Can you admit that you don't have all the answers?

Our beliefs become our future reality. Beliefs powerfully direct creation. That is how fortune tellers operate. They plant a seed by suggesting an idea for you to believe in. And if you choose to believe them, the outcome can emerge from the power of your belief.

As we encounter new information, we have blinders on. That is, we are not open to opposing our own views or beliefs. "I'm right, and you're wrong!" Being open-minded requires humility in acknowledging that you don't know what you don't know.

If You Believe Something, Does That Make It Real?

Whatever you believe is real. Period. If you believe in it, it exists. Do you believe in Santa Claus? Okay, then he's real. My daughter is seven years old as I write this. I thought perhaps she would stop believing in Santa this year. But right before Christmas, she said to me, "A boy in my class said there is no Santa Claus. So, I said to him, 'Well, there's not if you don't believe in him. But I *do* believe in him.' So, I told the boy, 'Yes, there *is* a Santa Claus.'"

I smiled.

Knowledge Comes from Opinions, Facts, and Personal Experiences

How much do you know so far? What percentage is that of everything that can be known? One percent? Fifty percent? One hundred percent?

I was laughing at myself recently when I went to my doctor to get a physical. My blood work came back with high cholesterol.

Well, it so happens that I had just read a book by a doctor who talked about how high cholesterol is actually good for your brain and not as bad for your heart as we've been told. I said to my doctor, "I know that cholesterol is a good thing for my brain because I read this book." The doctor smirked and looked away, probably thinking to himself, *Great. This guy has read a book by a doctor, and now he thinks he's a doctor, too.* Yes, I am a doctor now. Ha-ha! I've read a book or an article on the internet, and now I have all the facts! Sure. Most of us are experts after reading an opinion article on the internet. Right?

Making Decisions and Judgments Based on Very Limited Information and Experience

We all make judgments with limited information and experiences on many topics, including religion and politics. We are quick to make black-and-white judgments, and then defend our position. Is it worth it to always be right? Especially when the "right" we defend is based on limited information and experience, or the opinions and influence of others?

What Is Truth?

***Truth* defined:**
*   *That which is in accordance with fact or reality.*

Spiritually speaking, the truth always supports benefiting the greater good. The truth does not support selfish motives as an objective. The truth supports service to others, the greater good, and benefits everyone, not just some.

11

Faith Is Trust

***Faith* defined:**

- *Complete trust or confidence in someone or something.*
- *Strong belief in God or in the doctrines of a religion, based on spiritual enlightenment rather than proof.*

Blind people do not see the moon with their eyes, but still believe it's there. Why? Because others who can see it tell them to believe? Do we have to touch something or see it ourselves to believe that it exists, or can we believe in it based on another's testimony? We can believe without seeing, but that involves trust. And trust means having faith.

Chapter 3:
Explaining God

A Light Bulb Analogy

A light bulb produces light powered by electricity. Our body is the bulb, our consciousness is the light, and God is the electricity.

Consciousness Versus Conscience

Consciousness defined:
- *The state of being awake and aware of one's surroundings.*

Some people say that consciousness is physical; others say that it is nonphysical. There are many detailed theories supporting both views, but there is no definite consensus.

Human consciousness, or awareness as we know it, is dependent on our human senses to operate. It is a temporary reality, which consists of an experience of five senses, but it shapes the eternal part of us, which is the Great Spirit of One.

The Great Spirit of One is an eternal awareness that is *not* limited to a consciousness made up of five senses. The greater reality consists of completely unlimited awareness, unbound by senses, which is an unrestricted consciousness on a grand scale.

Conscience **defined:**

- *An inner feeling or voice viewed as acting as a guide to the rightness or wrongness of one's behavior.*

Your conscience can also be called your heart's will, God's will, or Spirit's will. It is an external influence upon our free will that directs us to make choices that benefit the greater good.

Projecting Our Human Perspective onto Our Definitions of "God"

We project our human experience, senses, and reality onto our concepts, ideas, and definitions of what God must be. In doing so, we imagine God as a big invisible human deity who exists somewhere else, with a human personality, emotions, and senses.

The Great Spirit of One—the eternal primary source of all life—wants to express itself through humans. But for that to occur, we must surrender our human nature, our temporary self or ego's will, to the eternal Spirit's will, which is also called God's will or our heart's will. We must deny the will of our temporary physical "self," "flesh," and "ego"—our instinctual and hormonal wills that direct us to be selfish, unforgiving, revengeful, cruel, greedy, and intolerant, fighting and harming others.

The Illusion of Separation Hides the Fact That We Are One

It is an illusion that we are individuals. In our human reality, which is based on five senses, we appear to be individuals. But in the greater reality unlimited by our five human senses, we are all One in spirit. That is hard to grasp when we are experiencing the human condition, because we look around and see all these other humans and other forms of life that appear separate. But the illusion is required for us to experience life as we do, for it to have the weight and meaning that it does for us. The illusion of being separate and individual begins at the time of our birth and continues forward throughout our experience until we physically perish. After we are born, we are given a name, and we develop memories containing our free-will choices throughout life. That experience creates a logical argument that we are all individual beings separated by space and wills. Logic says, "I am not you. You and I have different names and experiences. Logically, how can we be One, when we appear as many?"

We are born with amnesia, so that we do not know or fully understand that we are all part of One.

The illusion of separateness is necessary to give each of us free will. If we did not have free will, our experience of life would not be the same. Free will—in other words, our illusion of separateness—allows us choice, and that in turn creates the mystery, the unknown, and the potential of life, making the quality of everything we experience more meaningful.

We need the illusion of separateness from each other in order to experience life here as we do, for the One to interact with itself. The greater reality is that we are really just playing with ourselves. It may be bizarre to recognize this at first, because while we are in our human condition, the thought of letting go of our identity or ego is the last thing our "self" wants to do.

Think about this: we have no problem with make-believe when we entertain ourselves. We are willing to watch movies, to believe them as if they were true, and not think about the fact that we are just watching actors following scripts. To constantly remember that we are watching actors would spoil the movie. Also, do you want to see or hear the movie's ending before you watch it? No, the movie will not be as good when you already know what's going to happen. We like the mystery, the unknown, and the challenge.

Under the spell of our human amnesia, faith is required. We need more clarity about the truth that we are ultimately One to help us awaken and evolve as humans. But some parts of the truth will always remain a mystery beyond our understanding to keep the epic movie of life on Earth entertaining, and to keep free will and choice alive. "God" has remained hidden and elusive from itself in order to experience life and creation here as humans with individual free will.

We are not meant to know and understand everything. There will always be mystery, which makes life more interesting. For example, how did something start from nothing in the beginning? Or which came first, the chicken or the egg?

Somehow, life starts in some form, in the tiniest speck. Then that speck expands and grows, becoming whatever it wants. But what does it want? Look around. It's what you see. It's us. It's my cat. It's global coral spawning as a synchronized event during a specific moon cycle that occurs at the exact same time once every year.

God, the Great Spirit of One, has different shapes, dimensions, illusions, and expressions.

Our experience here as human beings is brief. Our ego's experience of the five senses is currently one of billions. The human shell comes and goes. And that's okay. But our spirit is and always will be forever part of an eternal whole. I was grateful to be reminded of this truth when it was revealed to me.

The illusion of separation according to our senses and logic constantly challenges and disputes the hidden truth that we need to understand in order to evolve as humans. Yes, this life is a challenge, and is meant to be. We do like challenges, don't we?

Human beings have free will and choice under the illusion that we are separate individuals here on Earth. Our eternal spirit guides us through our heart if we allow it, but that guidance is up against stronger influences—namely, our powerful, selfish survival instincts.

Our true identity is hidden from us while we have this human experience. Our evolution requires becoming more aware of what we truly are, or at least to develop more faith in the truth, which encourages us to become less selfish despite our challenges and ignorance.

There will always be another story to play out, with new characters and a new ending—always, forever, in more ways than you and I can imagine with our limited awareness. That is good news, not sad or scary news. This experience is an evolution of the combined choices of a whole that appears to be composed of separate parts.

The Spirit of One appears to be separated into different parts for different periods of time here on Earth. All forms of life are animated from this Spirit. Deep down we know this, but it is our challenge to develop experiences that increase clarity about this truth, and then maintain it.

God chooses to hide from itself, to create unique experiences—such as us. All life, although appearing separate, is a continuous ongoing creation of what is really one singular event and experience.

Ignore Logic to Proceed

We can do almost anything we want because we have free will, but we will pay a price for every choice we make. I am not referring here to human laws, which we can sometimes break without suffering consequences. There are spiritual laws that cannot be cheated or avoided. Spiritual laws always have consequences, positive or negative, rewarding or painful, regarding all of our choices. Whatever ripple we send out will come back to us in equal measure. Sooner or later, the return will come. When we are no longer ignorant of this truth, many of us will choose not to harm others. Or when we do, it will not be done ignorantly.

The truth is that beyond appearance and logic, I am you. Therefore, helping you is helping me. Our ego's identity of self perpetuates the denial of this truth—the truth that you and I are One, and not really individuals, as we appear to be. The lie is what our eyes tell us: that we are separate entities. We believe that illusion because it *appears* to be so. But things are not as they appear. That is why, when we harm others, we are ultimately harming ourselves. And because of that, when we harm others, we are unhappy and often lead unsatisfied lives with varying degrees of pain and suffering as a consequence of our ignorance. The pain is there to direct us toward making different choices that will reward us instead of hurting us, in order to help us see and understand this deeper truth beyond appearances.

Once we choose to operate based on the deeper truth beyond logic and appearances, the pain—the hell—dissolves, because the deeper truth is that we are all One spiritually. When I look into your eyes, the greater truth is that I am looking into my own eyes. This truth is hidden from us, and needs to be discovered and experienced by each individual. Discovering and experiencing this truth is called a spiritual awakening.

Faith Is Always Required Because Awakenings Become Memories

Although I was shown, with complete clarity, the truth of what we are in a series of revelations in January 2018, it was still just one singular event in time. Every event we experience becomes a memory—and over time memories fade. So based on my experience, even if we have complete clarity on truth in a singular event, the memory of that truth does fade over time.

Logical reality and the persistent ongoing illusion of separation are powerful forces. Faith is required when memories of awakenings and experiences of the truth fade, because our instincts, ego, and logic constantly promote denial of the greater truth. Spiritual awakenings are not permanent. They need to be maintained. There is no spiritual graduation.

Ignorance Causes Conflict

Resistance to being open-minded about spirituality and religion is very common. People get fired up and willing to argue when they start talking about religion or God. Should anyone argue or make war over religion or God? No. But when people think they're right and that they have the truth, some become willing to kill others with opposing views. Many people throughout history have wanted to force their versions of religion onto others. Christianity and Islam have both been guilty of this. But no one likes to be told what to do. Not realizing that, on a deep level, we are all One is at the root of this problem.

I Am

I am. You are. We are. Think about that. We usually take our life for granted, unless faced with a terminal diagnosis. No matter what your circumstances, your feelings, or your emotions right now, you exist. The impossible *is* happening.

I asked my Google Assistant on my cell phone to define *I Am*. The first definitions that came up were:

1. *God, seen as self-sufficient and self-existent.*
2. *A self-centered, arrogant person.*

Would you have guessed that the first definition of *I Am* on Google would be God?

Truth—You Know It When You Hear It

The truth rings a bell inside when you hear it. It's just a reminder of what you already knew deep down inside that you have forgotten.

God Is…

God is on, not off.

God is the energy and spirit of all life.

God is creation and creative.

God is the intelligence and orchestration for the good and benefit of all, forever.

God is unconditionally giving and unconditionally forgiving.

God is the parent of our parents.

God is every race and culture on the planet.

God is consciousness in every form.

God is the One Great Spirit.

God is forever changing, never destroyed.

God is infinite.

God is whatever it wants to be, unlimited and always.

God is the more than eight million species on this planet, including ours.

God is unity.

God is One, appearing as many.

Stop Ignoring the Suffering on Earth

Six months after my primary revelations, I had a brief second revelation. I was given a mass-level awareness of all the pain and confusion that exist in this world right now. It broke my heart in an indescribable way. I wasn't shown the pain of just a few people, but a glimpse into the entirety of pain, suffering, and confusion throughout the planet. That experience was followed by an overwhelming feeling of empathy. I didn't want that experience, but I understand why it happened. It gave me the drive I needed to complete this book.

For reasons of survival, a human being's default nature is to be selfish—to ignore the suffering around us in the world. Our selfish instinctual natures do not want to think about the suffering of others, because we don't want to be obliged to help, although we may feel guilty for not helping if that is brought to our attention. The human default is to actively avoid focusing on the suffering of others.

Each of us is connected to all other life on Earth. When there is pain or imbalance on the other side of the world, even though you don't see it and are unaware of it, you feel it deep down on

21

some level, because all life on this planet is connected spiritually. The healing begins with seeking and noticing who needs help—and then helping them.

Free Will Has Consequences

We have free will, which means we have the ability to make choices. We are not forced to choose a certain way, but how we choose will have consequences.

Why did Hitler kill all of those Jewish people? Why did God allow that?

Well, God did allow it. But God didn't choose to do it. Hitler had free will, and he chose to do it with *his* free will. He also convinced a lot of other people to follow him with their free will. Did Hitler have consequences, and did the people who followed him and made all those horrific choices have negative consequences? Yes, they did—seen and unseen.

You can do anything you want, so long as you are willing to pay the price. There is always a price, regardless of whether it is apparent or not. Consequences are positive or negative, based on the choices we make. What we give is what we get. That's the cycle. Consequences may be instant or delayed. They may be seen by others or unseen. But consequences are inescapable, regardless of belief. Nevertheless, God is not to blame for the consequences of the free-will choices made by humans.

Our Painful Experiences Can Be
Used to Help Others Later

What happens in this human life is just temporary—a singular blip in time. Every human being experiences suffering on different levels. But often the painful things that happen are later recycled in a way that can benefit others. For example, our own personal experiences with suffering can be used to relate to others, helping them with similar memories and experiences. Individuals who have been through difficult or painful experiences, who have found hope and acceptance on the other side of the issue, can be there for others with the same or similar past experiences in a way that others without the experience or memory cannot. Thus, our bad memories and experiences can be used to help others. A person who has gone through something painful, and then moved past it, can provide hope and support to someone with a similar loss or painful experience. Having support from others who can relate to our painful trials from their own experience is our greatest aid during difficult times.

We sometimes have painful or harmful experiences because of choices made by another person's free will. However, we can also have other painful experiences that don't have anything to do with another person's free-will choices, but are just part of the challenge and risk of human life, such as accidents, disasters, or terminal health issues. But all pain is temporary. Our pain, suffering, and challenges give a deeper meaning to the joy, beauty, appreciation, love, and gratitude in life. Yin and Yang. Both must exist to give the other deeper meaning.

Each of us has free will, which means that we get to decide, choose, and evolve for ourselves. The One divided itself up into us—parts that have forgotten who we truly are in order to experience itself. Seeds of desire to love one another were planted inside each of us to help steer our choices toward overcoming selfish instinctual desires during this unique human life experience. This loving guidance exists even in the most evil or selfish persons.

Yes, it may be walled off, hidden in complete denial, and buried a thousand miles below the surface, but it's there—an "implant to love." My message is to remind you that you don't know or remember how special you truly are. You may have had a horrible upbringing, neglectful or cruel parents, and a history of abuse from others, and yet, I want to say this to you: God did not do any of that to you. No. Being exposed to others' free-will choices that harmed you, just as being affected by disaster, accident, or disease, is part of the human life experience and challenge. It is the price we pay for free will and participating here as humans.

Why do some people choose to cause pain to others? Perhaps because that was done to them. Or perhaps not. One thing is clear: the people who hurt others are not happy, and they will ultimately pay for their choices with pain. Hell is here on Earth—it is the price one pays for choosing to harm others. Our challenge is to choose love and service, although we may have been abused and harmed by others.

Chapter 4:
Needs—Instinctual Drives

Maslow's Hierarchy of Needs

Abraham Maslow was an American psychologist in the last century, who came up with a list that ranks human needs in order of priority. Maslow's theory is that an individual's basic needs must be met before they become motivated to achieve higher-level needs.

The bottom of the pyramid contains the first level of our needs: the Physiological Needs. These lowest-level needs are necessary for our physical survival: food, water, breathing, shelter, clothing, sleep, sex, and homeostasis. This lowest level of needs is self-centered to ensure our individual survival and the survival of the species. Notice that sex is listed on this lowest level of our needs. I emphasize later how sex is one of our strongest instinctual drives influencing our motives.

Once the physiological needs are met, people can focus on their Safety and Security needs. This level refers to our need for financial security, personal security (health and physical safety), and emotional security. Everyone wants to feel secure and safe from harm. If our safety and security needs are taken away or threatened by war, natural disasters, family violence, or childhood

Figure 1: Maslow's Hierarchy of Needs

abuse, that can lead to Post-Traumatic Stress Disorder and chronic anxiety. People generally seek getting their needs for safety and security being met before focusing on any of the higher-level needs. Economic crisis and lack of work opportunities affect our financial security needs. Throughout this book, I sometimes refer to financial security needs as "money," which can also be viewed as our desire for resources that enable our survival. I refer to the financial security need for money as a powerful driver behind our motivations and choices. As described above, there are different types of needs/instincts associated with security, but financial security is the one I focus on most, because it is the one that most promotes selfishness.

After the first two levels of needs are met, we can begin to focus on the higher levels of needs. The third level of our needs is for Social Belonging and Love. This need can override the need for safety, as when children cling to abusive parents or victims stay

26

with their domestic violence abusers. Social belonging includes friendships, family, social groups, and romantic attachments. Some reasons that people do not get these needs met include hospitalization, neglect, shunning, or ostracism. Humans need to feel a sense of belonging and acceptance among small or large social groups. Some examples of large social groups are co-workers, religious communities, sports teams, and gangs. Some examples of small social groups are families, intimate partners, mentors, colleagues, and confidants. Humans need to love and be loved by others. In the absence of love and belonging, people experience depression, isolation, and social anxiety.

The fourth level of needs is Esteem, which is respect and admiration. Self-esteem is self-respect and admiration, which comes from giving and being of service to others, not just ourselves. Maslow describes a lower and higher version of esteem. The lower version is the need for others to respect and admire us. The higher version is the need to be respected and admired by ourselves.

According to Maslow, the fifth and highest level of needs is Self-Actualization, or, in his words, "the full realization of one's potential, and of one's 'true self.'"

Self-actualization is to fulfill our meaning and purpose in life. To find meaning, we must find our purpose, which is defined as how we can best use our unique talents and skills to serve everything and everyone around us. It is to find and practice how can we best benefit and contribute to the greater good.

Needs = Instinctual Drives

The needs can also be called instinctual drives, with the terms becoming interchangeable. The primary lower-level needs are self-centered, whereas the higher-level needs are other-centered. There are some basic primary physical needs that have no "off" switch. They drive us to always seek more, regardless of how much we already have. The two most dominant of these needs, or instinctual drives, are sex and financial security (money). I focus on these two needs, or instinctual drives, which are found in the first two levels of Maslow's Hierarchy, as the primary drivers of our self-centered behaviors. These are the two primary needs/ instincts that cause us to justify harming or neglecting others. To move up in the hierarchy of needs to esteem and self-actualization requires a conscious effort to shift away from focusing on self-centered physical needs, and toward needs that involve community and service to others.

Our Needs for Sex and Financial Security (Money)
Are the Primary Drivers Behind Our Selfishness

***Instinct* defined:**
- *A largely inheritable and unalterable tendency of an organism to make a complex and specific response to environmental stimuli without involving reason.*
- *A natural or intuitive way of acting or thinking.*
- *Behavior that is mediated by reactions below the conscious level.*

Instincts are our hard wiring, our preprogramming. Instincts can also be defined as our needs or desires in some cases. Again, I am focusing on the two most powerful and challenging of our hard-wired drives, which are the instinctual drives for sex and financial security (money). These two most powerful instinctual

28

drives strongly influence our free-will choices below the conscious level. These drives are selfish. Some selfishness is necessary for our survival. But when it dominates and controls our decisions and focus, we have problems. Managing these two powerful instincts is required for us to evolve.

Life Is Stressful When Physiological Needs Are Not Met or Are Threatened

We all experience stress when our basic needs for food and shelter are lost or threatened, and we also feel the relief that money brings by lowering the stresses that accompany poverty. Naturally, we assume that more money will bring even greater degrees of relief. However, our instincts for financial security are insatiable. We tell ourselves that "getting more" will be the solution to our discontent and unhappiness. But satisfaction is not attained by getting more for ourselves. To the contrary, satisfaction is attained by doing the complete opposite—namely, giving more and being of service to others, helping them to meet their needs. Throughout this book, I will be referring to these two dominant selfish needs of sex and financial security (money) as instinctual drives.

How Much Money Is Enough?

How much money do I really need? How much is enough? Well, if my instinctual drive for financial security (money) answers that question, there is *never* enough. I have experienced the stress of not having enough money to cover my basic needs for food and shelter. I have also had the relief of having enough money to *not* have to worry about those basic needs. My experience has shown me that once my basic needs are met, my ability to acquire more stuff does not add to my overall happiness and satisfaction with life. Because of our instincts for financial security, even once our basic needs are met, we live under the illusion that more money will increase our overall contentment and satisfaction with life.

Our instincts for financial security will always tell us that it is not smart or safe to give to others. Our instincts will always justify keeping more for ourselves. The lie is that the farther I am away from the stresses of poverty, the more content I will be. If given free rein, our instincts for financial security will always justify selfishness.

The stress of not having basic needs met is real. Many of us believe that having more money will eventually fix us, bringing us the happiness that we lack now. Many of us cannot give to others because our instincts tell us that we still need to get more before we can give anything away. That is why we feel the need to keep getting more, and more, and more. We may do some giving, but we usually keep most of what we obtain for ourselves. We think that having more will give us what we're searching for—but it won't. Beyond meeting our basic needs for food and shelter, hoarding wealth will not provide a deeper sense of purpose or well-being. In our selfish pursuit of more for ourselves, we are taken farther away from authentic connections with others. Being of service to others is what is required to obtain the real peace and joy that we seek.

Our instincts for financial security will always say, "We just don't have enough to give right now." And that is true, no matter how much we actually have. Our instinct for financial security promotes and encourages selfish hoarding. The more money we have, the stronger the tendency is to hold on to it, and the stronger the fear is of losing it.

Finding a Balance Between Saving and Hoarding

As our current societies function, we do need money to provide for our present and future needs. But the question is, *how much money?* In an ideal world, we would live on our "daily bread." But this attitude and action can, and usually does, put a burden on others to provide for us. The norm is for parents to provide for their children. But once those children become adults, unless they are disabled, expecting others to provide for them is selfish. It is selfish to expect others to take care of us when we haven't earned or saved anything to provide for ourselves. Circumstances can change suddenly, so we should be prepared for emergencies. It is responsible to have a prudent financial reserve to cover personal expenses for some time into the future. But how much is necessary? The goal is to find a balance between responsible saving and selfish hoarding. That is a question for all individuals to examine and decide for themselves.

Asking Others for Money

How often do you ask others to lend or give you money? If you do that consistently, whether it's once a month or every six months, that can be a sign of selfishness—or at least of poor money management. If you borrow the money, do you pay it back in a timely fashion, or at all? You may be living beyond your means, or pursuing too extravagant a lifestyle, expecting others to foot your bills. Your goal should be to live within your means, keeping a prudent reserve to help yourself in emergency times. When you ask others for money, you are asking them to make sacrifices for you. Are you willing to make sacrifices for others, or do you expect others to continually make sacrifices for you?

Inheritance Can Be a Curse

We have heard that the love of money is the root of all evil. After my dad died, I received an inheritance. Money can bring out greed in people when it comes to who gets what from an inheritance, and that greed for money can tear families apart. Sometimes they heal later, but sometimes not. My inheritance separated me from those in my family who were left out. It's sad how selfish, greedy, and foolish our instincts can make us behave over money.

Can Money Buy Love?

Money can buy "pretend," temporary, conditional love—but it cannot buy real, unconditional, lasting love.

Money cannot buy time, peace, health, character, integrity, or true friends.

If You Could Be Granted Any Wish, What Would It Be?

What's the first thing that comes to mind? Is the answer something selfish, or is it something beyond yourself for the greater good? Our default mode is to be selfish.

Lottery Winners

A classic question is: "If you won a multimillion-dollar lottery, what would you do?" Usually, the responses are selfish. "Oh, I want this, I want that. I want a car. I want a vacation. I want, I want, I want." It's always me, me, me. Not many people will say, "I want to help poor people and give to others who are in need or suffering in some way." Who says that? Practically no one.

Have you ever prayed to win the lottery and bargained with God by promising that you would help people if you won? Meanwhile, deep down, you knew you wouldn't follow through, or at least not as much as you promised to God. And then you immediately felt guilty because of that thought. You always knew you wouldn't win, because your underlying thoughts were selfish.

"If I won the lottery," you say, "that would solve all my problems, and I'd be so happy."

But would you? If you won the lottery, would you be a giver or a taker? When we examine the history of lottery winners, we discover that many spend it all and go broke in a relatively short period of time. Why? Because they use the money to try to make themselves happy, rather than to benefit or help others. In addition to losing the money, they usually also lose their "friends," who disappear as soon as the money runs out.

Happiness Is in the Future Once I Get...

Most of us have a persistent belief that we will find happiness sometime in the future, once we obtain some relationship, possession, or goal. "I would be happy," we say, "if I could only get a new partner, or get married, or own a home, or graduate, or go on a vacation, or decorate my house, or start a hobby, or get the job I desire, or get a new car." But all those things come and go, and they don't give us the feeling we expected, or the excited feelings don't last very long. Then it's, "Okay, what's next?" And we remain a hamster on the treadmill.

Happiness Is Not a Choice

I just read a post on Facebook in which someone said, "Happiness is a choice."

I responded, "Happiness is a byproduct and the result of the actions of giving to others unconditionally."

Happiness is *not* a choice. At least, it is not a direct choice. It is an indirect choice that results from unconditional giving. Being unselfish earns the positive consequence of happiness. There is no on-and-off switch for happiness. Sure, we would love to have one, so that we could be happy with no effort and no sacrifice. But that kind of thinking is the root cause of the problem of our being unhappy in the first place—because it is selfish and self-centered. It's wanting something for nothing all the time—all take, no give. When we seek to control our happiness by using alcohol or drugs, the consequences are usually negative, if not devastating. Instincts and self-centeredness have to be consistently overcome and managed for us to get the happiness we desire through giving and an others-centered lifestyle.

The selfish gratification pleasures that we chase tend to fade quickly. And then we say, "I need it again. I need more. I want more. I'm never satisfied."

When you are living that way, you are in a state of constant restlessness and irritability. It's like being stuck in a cycle of hell—no peace, no satisfaction, no rest.

You're never pleased with what you have, with where you are, or with what you're doing. You always think that if you can change the scene and go somewhere else, or be with someone else, or get something else, then you will be satisfied and happy. That's a lie. It's an illusion. It's living in denial of the truth. What we are seeking is bliss, peace, joy, and happiness. The problem is that those feelings do *not* come from getting, from pleasure, or from self-gratification.

Once you have done enough unconditional giving, you will obtain a deep, lingering peace, a feeling that all will be fine, regardless of circumstances. That peace will allow you to start breaking free of the need for instant gratification, which is the nonstop attempt to maintain a fading buzz of some sort.

I'll Be Happy When I Get More….

Will getting more make you happy? In my late twenties, I made more money than I ever had before—way more than I needed to cover my basic needs. But I became more selfish than I had ever been. Why was that? I gave less when I had more. Why? For me, having more didn't make me feel happy, so I thought, *I don't have enough yet.* I used that logic to justify being greedy. Then my instincts kicked in with lies that told me, "I still need more," and "If I get more, then I'll be happy." Because happy hadn't happened yet.

But that's the lie. More is *never* enough. There's no amount of money or stuff that will ring the "happy" bell, because happiness does *not* come from getting—it comes as a byproduct of giving. At the time, I had more to give, but I didn't give it to experience the happiness I was seeking, because my instincts were dominating and controlling me.

If I only had a new Corvette, I told myself, *I would be happy.* So I got one. The excitement lasted for about three months—but that was excitement, not happiness. I was not closer or more connected to other people as a result of getting that car. People did not like me more because I had that car. In fact, I sensed envy and jealousy from others because of that car. Having that Corvette did not bring me closer to others, as I had falsely imagined it would. Sure, the car was fun to drive, but that fun faded over a short time, and then I was looking for another source of fun and excitement.

The same pattern has repeated over and over with my romantic relationships, since I always sought something new and different for excitement. The newness that brings the unknown, mystery, and excitement always fades over time. Chasing novelty can be entertaining, but it gets old fast. Getting anything or anyone is only a brief distraction that starts to fade soon after the first encounter. Furthermore, the fantasy of the chase is never the reality. Seeking something or someone to fill a craving is to remain in a perpetually dissatisfied state of suffering—as Buddhism says. To restate the truth, any mindset that revolves around "getting" to make me happy will only turn out to disappoint me. True happiness is a byproduct of giving, not getting.

Instant Gratification Versus Delayed Gratification

Our instinctual programming for survival and selfishness is much stronger than the whispers of our heart, which tell us to deny ourselves, love one another, and serve and sacrifice for others. Our instinctual demands versus our heart's whispers create a constant never-ending battle between them. Some people label this fight "flesh versus spirit." The heart's guidance system directs us to give and love, but it is only a faint whisper compared to the shouting, screaming demands of the instinctual drives, which want instant gratification.

The heart's desires usually involve self-sacrifice and delayed

36

gratification, which are not directed by the instinct-based, immature, instant gratification of getting a selfish pleasure satisfied at the moment. The instant-gratification feelings that come from getting something new, or sex, or drugs fade quickly. The heart is patient and wiser, wanting the deeper, more constant feelings of happiness, peace, and joy, which are earned by the delayed gratification of unconditionally giving over time.

Instincts: Sex, Sex, and More Sex...

Why do we want sex? The obvious primary purpose of sex is for us to procreate. There is also a selfish-pleasure reward component. But what fundamentally drives this powerful urge, this instinctual drive in humans?

The sexual urge in humans, both male and female, is primarily driven by the hormone testosterone. Most people know that testosterone is the primary male trait-influencer hormone. But *both* sexes require this hormone to have a sex drive. Without testosterone, neither gender would desire sex. On average, men have levels of testosterone up to thirty times higher than women do. That is why men have a much higher sex drive in general than women. According to healthline.com, for men over 19, normal testosterone levels range between 240 and 950 nanograms per deciliter. For women over 19, normal testosterone levels range between 8 and 60 nanograms per deciliter.

I took testosterone supplements for two years, so I have had personal experience with increasing and then decreasing it in my system. A couple of years ago, I decided to join the new fad of testosterone supplements with the intent of having more energy, increasing strength, losing waist fat, and gaining muscle. My levels went from 280 to 700 nanograms per deciliter—more than double my normal levels at the time, which supposedly put me back to the testosterone level of a 20-year-old male.

Doubling my testosterone level increased my strength, muscle mass, ambition, and sexual drive. But the increased testosterone also increased my feelings of anger and aggression.

After being on testosterone supplements for over a year, I decided to stop them. Then I learned that after ceasing testosterone supplements, the body can take up to a year to produce natural levels again. A month after I stopped taking the supplements, my blood level of testosterone dropped from 700 to 37 nanograms per deciliter. My doctor said that that was the lowest level he had ever seen for a male. At that extremely low level, my sex drive completely disappeared. I was like a child before puberty, with no sexual desires, urges, or thoughts. It was a return to innocence. I actually didn't mind this at the time. It was a relief to be given a break from thinking about sex for a while.

What I didn't like about the lower levels of testosterone was the noticeable decline in physical strength and an overall decrease in ambitious drive. I also didn't like feeling fear on greater levels, and feeling more emotionally sensitive.

I have watched nature documentaries that show male elephants, seals, and elk during mating season, with their high testosterone levels urging them to fight, gouge, and even kill each other for access to females. This behavior is prompted solely by testosterone. All those male animals are violently competing for the right to mate and spread their genes.

Testosterone is the hormone that drives procreation in the human species and many others. But it not only has driven procreation, it has also enabled man's drive to hunt and kill for survival.

Because men have much higher levels of testosterone than do women, they commit the majority of violent and sexual assaults. Testosterone challenges our evolution, which will require choosing *not* to fight or to react in anger, regardless of our hormonal-driven feelings to do so.

Human Partnership Is Usually a Conditional Trade for Sex and Financial Security

Generally speaking, in intimate partnerships, women instinctually seek financial security and protection, whereas men seek sexual satisfaction. These are primary traditional instinctually driven roles for each gender. There are other roles as well, which can vary, but overall these dominate and make it easy to see where financial security and sex motivate the strings-attached trades in intimate partnerships. I have also observed these instinctually motivated roles in homosexual relationships, in which one partner provides the masculine financial security and protection role, and the other provides the sexual feminine role.

Usually, when one side in a partnership stops providing the expected role, resentment and anger arise, which often leads to separation. For example, if breadwinners lose their job or become unable to provide financial security, their partner will probably resent that and seek a new a partner who *can* provide. The same is true if sex is no longer provided by one of the parties.

The inability to provide financial security and sex can happen to either party in a relationship due to health problems or random unforeseen changes. That is when it becomes clear whether or not the other partner can still love unconditionally. Many cannot, which is why there is so much divorce.

We see these instinctual pitfalls when a woman chooses a partner based on financial security instead of attraction, which is a recipe for unhappiness from the beginning. Similarly, if a man chooses a partner primarily based on sexual attraction, ignoring or overlooking glaring incompatibilities, he is embracing sabotage from the beginning. Sex and financial security are conditional components in many intimate relationships.

Chapter 5:
Nature Is Balanced

The Perfect Circle of Giving and Receiving in Nature

The lion or lioness that kills to eat, or to feed the cubs, or to feed others in the pride, is part of a repeating cycle of giving and receiving. The animal that is killed is giving itself as nutrition to another animal that is receiving. The transformation and continuation of life occurring through matter shifting form is the circle of life. Life gives to life over and over. One animal eats another, and then poops it out. The poop is fertilizer for the ground, becoming the food for plants that some other animals eat—a perfect, complex balance and design here on Earth. Plants produce the oxygen we breathe, while we produce the carbon dioxide they need.

Everything is connected. Everything has a reason and purpose. When we examine nature from our human perspective, it sometimes seems cruel, but it's all perfectly designed. There is a reason for every interaction that benefits the greater good.

When the lioness has cubs, and one of them gets sick, she stops feeding it and lets it die. Isn't that cruel? Why does she do it? To ensure the survival of the healthy ones. Nature respects limited resources, and so it makes the hard choices.

There is a species of large birds, called Shoebills, which look like ducks. They waddle around, but they can't fly. A male and female couple of this species was filmed in a documentary by the BBC in the Bangweulu Wetlands near Kananga, in northern Zambia, Africa. This species always has two chicks. One chick lives and the other dies every time. From the moment the chicks hatch, the parents decide to put all their energy into the stronger one. They feed it and nurture it, letting the weaker one starve to death. That is a choice they make with every birth.

Suffering occurs here on Earth. But it is temporary for every form of life. No suffering is forever. The pain that takes place, which we judge to be cruel, only occurs for a brief period. The suffering occurs for a variety of complex reasons, but the ultimate reason is the survival and continuation of all life. We are just beginning to study and understand some of the complicated reasons behind decisions in nature. Every choice in nature ultimately benefits the whole.

Life on Earth always has a beginning and an end. One dies for another to live. Everything is giving something in some way to something else. Life is a series of tradeoffs and transformations, with all life forms giving and benefiting through sacrifice. Everything gives to everything else, all the time. That's the balance—the way life is designed to be. Human beings are interrupting that process by taking more than we give, disrupting delicate give-and-take processes in the environment and in nature.

All life on Earth serves a purpose that is related to giving to the entire cycle of life. When you know a life form's purpose, you like it and you want it to exist because you understand why it is here and what it contributes. Every part of life on the planet is connected to you by an invisible line, whether or not you recognize

42

that connection. We are not separate from the planet or its life here.

Have you ever looked at a cat or a dog and thought about the similarities we share with them as life forms? We have the same five senses of sight, hearing, smell, touch, and taste. We all have two eyes, one nose, one mouth, and two ears on our heads, and organs with similar functions and arrangements. Then there are other life forms on the planet that are vastly different from us. For example, octopuses have three hearts and nine brains. Some life forms here don't share the senses we have, or they have other senses that we don't have, such as sonar in dolphins and bats or electricity in eels and stingrays.

There's so much we don't know or understand yet about all the life around us. But we do have fun discovering it and learning about it. Every time I watch a nature program on TV, I see some creature I've never heard of before. There are many other living species, such as plants, insects, and deep ocean life, that I can't even begin to relate to because they are so different from me. Because of that, do I value those forms of life less?

Every form of life is here on this planet for a reason, and every life is part of a perfectly balanced design of giving and receiving. Everything operates in synch for a greater good and a greater purpose, evolving to benefit the whole. We are constantly learning about the connections between all of life. Everything living here serves a purpose and benefits the whole in some way. All life is a cycle of giving and receiving, whether or not we yet understand all the connections. Receiving is not being selfish—*if* you are also giving. You receive so that your own needs are met, and so that you can continue giving.

But then there is us. Human beings have been disrupting this perfect balance in massive ways, because we have been ignorantly driven by instincts that make us selfish and inconsiderate of other forms of life. We are in denial about the depth of our true connection to other life on this planet. We ignore our negative impact on the planet, justifying our selfish behavior. The problem is that we humans are taking way too much, and producing more of ourselves to do more taking. It's simply unsustainable. Human beings are in denial about this truth. Some examples include overfishing the oceans, claiming dominion over more and more land, and overpopulating and polluting the planet.

I recently watched a documentary about an elephant family, which followed their lives over a ten-year period and revealed their intimate social bonds and complex relationships. I witnessed their ups and downs, how they communicate, how they interact with their babies and relatives, how they support each other, how they bond, and, finally, how they grieve loss. Elephants live for sixty to seventy years in the wild. When one dies, all of its brothers and sisters and aunts and uncles and children are sad and grieve. For a time, the family unit is disrupted. Why would anyone want to kill an elephant? A selfish supply-and-demand cycle drives killing elephants for their ivory. So long as there is demand, the supply will be obtained until it is depleted. People will only choose to stop because of spiritual enlightenment, or perhaps the legal consequences become too severe.

There are over eight million species of life forms on Earth, and all of them are dependent on and connected to all other life forms. We have the power to destroy it all, including ourselves— or not. Programmed guidelines direct most forms of life. Aside from humans, other life forms just seem to know what to do to share, interact, and remain in balance with the life forms around them. Humans, on the other hand, have an unregulated selfishness that other life forms lack, so that we take more than we give. But there is still time for us to salvage this experiment. We have been sabotaging a very delicately designed balance on Earth. Yet, there is still hope.

Chapter 6:
What We Give Is What We Get

Life Is a Boomerang

Over two thousand years ago, someone tried to tell mankind that life is a boomerang, but we haven't completely gotten it yet. It's a simple message that people have refused to believe: *What we give is what we get*. We reap what we sow. Whatever we put out will boomerang back to us over time. Not just in money, but also in how we treat others. In dealing with other people, the most important question to ask ourselves is, "How do I want to be treated by others?"

If you treat others with kindness, love, patience, tolerance, forgiveness, and generosity, that is what will come back to you later. If you are mean, angry, hateful, intolerant, unkind, unforgiving, or impatient, *that* will come back to you later. There are consequences for what you put out to the world, good or bad. It is easier to see the results of this truth in the lives of others. It is much harder to see it in our own lives and to connect the dots. That is especially true if what you have been giving to others has not been all that good. In that case, who wants to accept the responsibility for the negative returns? No one does. Your experience with life is generally a reflection of your own choices—that is, of what you have been giving to the world. This truth can be seen best in hindsight. It is a spiritual law that is revealed when it is honestly examined over time.

Yet, so many of us do not understand or believe the cause-and-effect principle of this truth. Many people can't or won't connect the dots to accept this truth as fact. Is the problem that we don't know how to be honest with ourselves and take responsibility for making choices that bring pain and suffering into our lives? Or is the problem that we see some people who hurt others appearing to get away with it, at least temporarily? Most people assume no personal accountability for their negative experiences, blaming the world for giving them back what they've put out. That mindset completely ignores the fact that the world's reactions to us are mostly a reflection of our own past and current behavior. Once we truly accept that this spiritual law applies, regardless of our beliefs, it will motivate us to stop hurting others.

Drug Dealers Say, "Someone Has to Supply the Demand"

Drug dealers make money off the addiction of others. They often justify this by stating that they are only satisfying a demand. A dealer says, "If *I* don't do it, somebody else will. So, why shouldn't I profit?"

Drug dealers justify selling drugs by blaming it on their customers. But the problem with that logic is ignorance. If you are harming others, enabling them to hurt themselves, you will pay a steep price down the road. If you are dealing drugs, you can tell yourself all kinds of excuses to justify making the money, but what are you really doing? You are participating in the destruction of people's health, families, and children. You are eliminating the user's ability to give to others, and the ripple effect is extremely negative. The price for this will be pain and suffering coming back to you indirectly or directly over time. Your actions have to be of a giving nature for your life to be good.

What I Dish Out Comes Back

When I get angry and hurt someone else, I look back on it after a few minutes and think, *Crap! Now I'm gonna get that back. Somehow, some way, I know it's coming back to me. It's guaranteed because it's a cycle..., unless I make amends right away.*

If I am feeling and expressing anger, and making someone else feel it, it will come back to me, sooner or later. When it does come back, if I can remember how I gave it out before, it's a little easier to take, because I know I had it coming. I'm just paying a fine that's coming due.

If You Give Insults, You Will Receive Insults

I recently saw someone's post on Facebook that he thought was funny. It showed a picture of a small card that someone had printed out and left on a car windshield. The card said, "You suck at parking. The next time this happens, I'm going to key your car. Fair warning."

I bet the person who had those cards printed for future use is getting back the same energy and attitude from others, not realizing that she (or he) is the problem and cause. Ignorance of this truth is the primary reason that people treat each other poorly. Do I want others to treat me with patience, tolerance, and kindness? If I do, I need to treat them with patience, tolerance, and kindness—especially when they are less than perfect.

Do You Get Away with Stealing If Nobody Sees It?

Stealing is the opposite of giving. It is taking what does not belong to you from other people without their permission. Some of us tell ourselves any number of lies to justify stealing. But regardless of justifications, those people will pay a price later. They will suffer for choosing to steal. And I'm not just talking about being caught and sent to jail. I'm saying that even if they are not caught by the police, they will pay internally. That is guaranteed.

It surprises me how many people are completely ignorant of that truth. The negative consequences that come later are meant to guide us into connecting the dots to understanding that truth. There is a price to pay for stealing, whether or not we are caught. So, we can never really "get away" with stealing. Ever. Even if no one else knows we did it.

The immediate benefit of stealing will be less than the punishment we pay later. There is no way around it. If we cheat others, we are only cheating ourselves in the future.

You must realize that you won't get any true joy from anything you have stolen. It is all tainted ill-gotten gains. You wonder why you are miserable, and why bad coincidences seem to happen to you, after you steal from others to "survive." You try to justify it in your mind, thinking that there is no price to pay if you don't get caught. But you will pay for it all eventually, whether you know that or not. That fate is guaranteed. Truth is not always what you want it to be.

I suggest that if you ever have the urge to steal something, instead give something of yours away. As soon as you have the urge, give your resources, time, and attention unconditionally to someone. Give instead of taking. There's another paradox for you.

Many times our answers to our questions are the complete opposite of what we expect.

If you have stolen in the past, how do you reverse what is coming back to you? How do you correct it and turn it around? First, stop stealing immediately. Second, give back everything you have stolen, ASAP, no excuses—anonymously if necessary. Start giving above and beyond your resources and time. What do you want your future to be like? Do you want happiness, peace, and joy?

You can always change your actions and start reversing them. You can start a good ripple effect at any moment. Otherwise, the feelings you desire will be absent and unavailable to you. It is never too late to start choosing a better future for yourself.

The Results of Making Money by Benefiting Others Versus by Harming Others

How do you make money? Money is usually traded for products or services that benefit others. But if you make money by cheating, stealing, or somehow harming others, then that money will bring you misery—meaning you will experience very little, if any, true happiness, peace, joy, or serenity. That is just the rule of the game, like it or not, know it or not.

If the way you get money involves hurting others, that hurt will come back to you. There is always a price to pay down the line for harming others. The price will be that the people and things you love and want around you will eventually be taken away. The passing pleasures and distractions that you can buy with the money made through harming others are fruits from a poisoned tree. Sooner or later, those distractions will stop covering the wave of pain you are putting out that is coming back to you.

No matter how much money you make, you are not going to be happy with it if the way you make it harms others. You will live a haunted life. Your sleep will have more nightmares than dreams. Peace and joy will completely elude you. You know the truth of this deep down inside. You are the only one who can change how you make your money, thereby changing the quality of your life and your future.

Chapter 7:
Unconditional Giving

Feelings from Unconditional Giving

It turns out that we only find true peace, serenity, and joy as a byproduct of being loving and giving with other people with the expectation of nothing in return. That is unconditional giving, which means doing something with no expectation of something in return, with no strings attached. Our fulfillment, our true happiness, is a byproduct of unconditionally giving.

Shortcuts are self-seeking pleasure and gratification for our selfish selves. Shortcuts are false and fleeting. Shortcuts provide what I call "minor" feelings. "Major" feelings include those with the highest quality attainable in the human condition: true happiness, peace, love, and joy. Those major feelings that we are all seeking only come from unconditional giving. That's it—that's the only way to get them. As we exercise our own free will, major feelings are earned by our choices that involve sacrifice and benefit for others. They don't come from getting or taking, from pleasures, or from self-gratification.

Giving unconditionally is not our "default" or what we "want" to do most of the time. It's up to us to start giving unconditionally when we don't want to. Our free will is influenced by the subtle whispers of our heart's will, and by the much louder will of our selfish instincts. Our instincts' will and influence are incredibly self-centered, whereas our heart's will is completely unselfish. Listening to the heart's will requires us to ignore the more powerful selfish will of the instincts, and then act against them. The goal is to increase our choices for serving others instead of only ourselves. And by doing that, we unlock the major feelings we all seek.

Unconditional giving is the only way to express love truly. It is the "action" of love. Giving unconditionally gets us unconditional love from others in return. We reap what we sow. However, timing isn't always immediate and apparent. Sometimes our gratification is delayed, rather than instant.

True love is unconditional, not conditional. Unconditional giving is giving with love because there are no strings attached. Conditional giving is giving without love because there *are* strings attached—a return motive, a give-and-take, an expected trade of some kind.

When you start unconditional giving consistently for a period of time, you will get wisdom and a depth of peace that you have never had before. You don't know what that feels like until you do. You cannot buy it. You cannot use money to buy the major feelings that the actions of unconditional giving bring to you. You simply cannot buy peace, serenity, or joy. They have to be earned over time through sacrifice and your choice to serve others instead of yourself.

Spiritual Awakenings Result from the Action of Unconditional Giving to Others Over Time

As a result of unconditional giving with no strings attached over a period of time, I began having a spiritual awakening. My spiritual awakening began from my choices and actions of giving to others unconditionally over time.

Six months prior to my revelations, because of my continued acts of unconditional giving, I began awakening to a peace, happiness, and joy that I had never known before. As part of that awakening, I began realizing that the Golden Rule was true because I noticed that the energy and resources that I gave out to others kept coming back to me.

The key to my spiritual experience and awakening was starting to practice the action of unconditional giving. The goal of Expert Giver Groups is to assist individuals with initiating and maintaining unconditional giving in their lives.

Unconditional giving over time results in the experience of becoming enlightened.

I didn't have to "get" or "understand" God in an intellectual way to have an awakening. A spiritual awakening does not result from learning information, but rather from choosing to give to others unconditionally and to forgive them over time. All that was necessary for me was to begin giving unconditionally, for a long enough period of time. Then I started to become aware of things that I didn't know before.

My spiritual awakening involved understanding the truth in life, which is normally hidden. It began with having moments of clarity in which I could see that what we give is what we get. I realized that if I help you, I'm really helping me. Furthermore, if you hurt, I hurt—even if you are on the other side of the world. Through the practice of unconditional giving, I was beginning to see through the persistent illusion that we are all separate individuals, and starting to see that we are all part of the same Spirit of One.

Some of us have heard that the answer to finding God is deep down within us, so we think, *Oh, I should meditate to find God within.* Yes, if we can achieve the complete release of our ego through meditation, that is certainly one method to glimpse the truth of the greater reality of One. But an initial experience with enlightenment can also result from choosing to start unconditionally giving to other people.

A spiritual experience can result as a byproduct of being of service to others unconditionally over time. It involves action—the action of giving. "Faith without works," says James 2:26, "is dead" (KJV). Knowledge in itself does not bring spiritual enlightenment. It is applied knowledge that matters. To be of service most effectively, the giving must be unconditional—with no strings attached, and with no motives for sex or money attached. Most of us give with an expected outcome in return. By his example, Jesus taught that unconditional giving is the answer—that is, giving with no return motive. If there is a motive behind the giving, we don't get the results we are seeking—which is unconditional giving coming back to us. If we give to others with strings attached, then others will give to us with strings attached. But if we give unconditionally to others, then others will give unconditionally back to us. That's how it works. Overall, we get exactly how we give over time. Our future reflects our ongoing choices.

What does it mean to be spiritual? It means to follow your heart. It is sacrifice and service to others, despite selfish desire, thereby gaining awareness of the insight that we are all truly One. That awareness does not come from religious traditions. Insight into spiritual truths come from giving unconditionally. The more you give, the more it is revealed to you that when you give to others, you are really giving to yourself.

In my case, I gave unconditionally for over six months. It was at the end of that period that I was unexpectedly shown my series of revelations, after which I understood that the previous six months of my unconditional giving had earned me the revelations. I became aware that I had unknowingly passed a test, and the reward was the revelations and the purposes I was given by the Spirit of One.

Continued Giving Is Required to Maintain a Spiritual Awakening

A spiritual awakening has to be maintained by continually giving to keep it. After we are awakened, if we relapse into letting selfish instinctual drives take over for too long, the awakening disappears, fading from memory like a dream that can eventually be forgotten altogether. That is, we can completely forget our previous spiritual awakenings if we fall back into just following our instincts, which will always continually promote selfishness, directing us only to take and not give.

Have you ever heard of individuals who had faith and then lost it? It is harder for those people to get their faith back than it is for those who never had faith to acquire it. It is very depressing to go from being a giver to a taker, without knowing or remembering how to get back to giving. The goal is to remain in giving cycles for longer and longer periods of time.

If I stop giving over time, I can forget how to give again. I can even forget that giving worked and how it felt—like a dream I cannot remember. That means forgetting the connection between giving and the peace, serenity, and joy that accompany it. How can I forget that? Because I have instinctual drives that are really powerful, and that will lie to me, and wipe out my memory of how to give and of all the positive results that are connected to my giving. I cannot rely on yesterday's giving to keep carrying me forward with continued levels of peace, serenity, and joy. I have to continue giving to maintain those feelings.

That is why accountability to another person, which requires humility, is important. Good friends will remind us that giving and serving are our solution here, and not selfish behavior or blaming others for our problems. Having the humility to become accountable to others for support with instinct management is part of the objective of Expert Giver Groups.

Once you have a spiritual awakening, it must be maintained daily through the continued action of unconditional giving. Otherwise, it becomes lost and forgotten. The process is comparable to exercising for keeping your body in shape.

Are Poor People the "Happiest"?

According to a documentary film called *Happy*, some of the poorest people in the world are the happiest. One part of the documentary is about people who live in huts with dirt floors in a village in India. They have severely limited supplies of food and clothing. But then I noticed something. They are all smiling. What do they have to be happy about? They are interconnected, and rely on each other. They are not isolated and alone. Social connections are an important ingredient for happiness.

On the other hand, in our complex society, we have online replacements for the real thing, isolating us further and further from each other. The trouble is, it's not working. The illusion is that we are connecting more, which we may be, but we are connecting more on superficial, not intimate or genuine levels. Happiness is only real when it is shared, not in isolation. We need more physical interaction with genuine connection and feedback from others, not more virtual interaction, which only provides and promotes more superficial connections and feedback.

In the United States, we are closely surrounded by thousands and even millions of people, but we are still feeling more and more alone, isolated, apart, and separate. With less genuine and intimate connection to other people, each of us is in our own little world—on our phones, our laptops, watching Netflix, trying to entertain and distract ourselves endlessly in isolation. Many of us look to drugs and medicines to fix us. But that doesn't work, either.

Life is better if we don't try to live it alone. We need support from and interactions with other people to enable the cycle of giving and receiving to and from others. Also, we benefit from others in the form of guidance, feedback, and accountability for helping us to grow in positive directions. Specifically, I am proposing to help and support others on our unconditional giving journeys by supporting, attending, and helping to develop Expert Giver Groups around the world. We are not meant to be isolated and to live alone, unconnected except on superficial levels. Participation and interaction through actual physical means involving honesty, being genuine, vulnerability, and trust are becoming a thing of the past. Visiting in person, and talking about what is really going on is happening less and less.

For me to love you, and for you to love me, we need to have a two-way relationship by interacting with each other, preferably in person and not electronically. Can we sit in public—or any-where—waiting for food or whatever for five minutes without looking at our phone, Facebook, Instagram, or the news? We have become distraction junkies, with our connections to others limited to hitting the "like" button or raging and venting about something online. We are stuck in a loop of media distractions. Streaming entertainment, internet content, social media, and our phones are consuming us. We are trapped in a loop of isolating and distracting ourselves. That has become the new norm. I'm guilty too. It's not easy not to fall into the phone or laptop distraction trap.

People treat each other very differently on social media than they do in person—especially in negative ways. We are more connected than ever with social media by the numbers, but it is generally on a superficial level. The online arena has caused more division, becoming a place to vent opinions and arguments, rather than a place of support and unity. Having supportive get-togethers to connect in person is becoming a rare event for many people these days. When I was growing up, I remember my dad regularly taking me to visit family members and friends. A common thing to do was actually to visit with people. These days, many of us don't know our neighbors.

We may be around lots of people physically during the day, but we are not connecting emotionally or being real. We are not touching; we are not hugging. And everyone is worried about behaving and keeping apart. Political correctness has exploded. Everyone is on guard, not trusting anyone, ready to fight or run. Even though many of us go to Starbucks every day, we are not talking to each other in line. We don't trust each other. We are scared of each other, and we limit the risks involved with interaction. We are just seeing each other and being physically near each other. We may share half a second of eye contact, but then it's back to the phone.

What's going on here?

What's going on is that we are all distracted, confused, and in pain on various levels, all the time. We are on guard. We rarely connect in person with each other on deep or intimate levels. Conversations usually go like this:

"How are you?"

"Fine. How are you?"

"Fine."

If we give a real response to that question, people are not ready for it. It's as if we broke the "keep it all superficial" rules. Many times our public connections involve quick smiles, darting eye contact, and awkward chitchat about the weather. We are usually glad when the conversation is over, so we can hurry back to our safe place of self-focused distractions. We lack meaningful connections and authentic interactions with others, emotionally, mentally, and physically. We are all yearning for deeper connections, but we have lost trust in each other, so we try to stay safe by remaining distant to protect ourselves from getting hurt. Intimate connection is not going to happen in line with strangers at Starbucks. We need to have a regular place to go with the intention of building authentic relationships with others we meet in person. My intent with Expert Giver Groups is to provide a meaningful, safe, and supportive way for us to reconnect again in person on a regular basis.

Happiness Is Only Real When It Is Shared

I recently saw a movie called *Into the Wild*, which tells a true story about a guy who goes on a journey by himself into the wilderness. The most significant thing that I remember from the movie is that he wrote in his journal about his search for happiness—which is, after all, the reason he spends all that time alone in the wilderness. What he discovers is that "happiness is only real when it's shared." It doesn't happen when we are by ourselves, alone, in isolation. We need each other to experience happiness.

That message was also given to me in my second revelation.

Self-Focus Is the Problem—Other-Focus Is the Solution

When a friend calls and starts to complain about self-centered problems, ask him what he is doing to help other people. Helping you helps me. I can get out of my own head and problems by helping someone else. In most cases, when I help others with their problems, my problems tend to resolve themselves.

Our primary goal in life should be to be other-focused, not self-focused. I was talking to a friend recently who is always focused on his own problems, and he is chronically depressed as a result. Focusing on ourselves and our own problems all the time *is* the problem. Our self-centeredness *is* the problem. Staying focused on "the problem" or "our problems" *is* the problem. But if I'm busy helping you, I'm not thinking about me.

Self-focus as a general operating mode is a primary reason for depression. The reason why we are chronically restless, irritable, and discontented is that we are completely self-centered most of the time, focused only on ourselves. Constantly analyzing ourselves is not going to solve our problems. The answer is not to call someone to talk about ourselves over and over or to continuously analyze ourselves. Self-analysis can be helpful, but only if its intent or focus is on helping me become more giving and less selfish with others. Focusing on others somehow helps us to solve our own problems, which in many cases start to magically take care of themselves. Sometimes trying to figure out the answer is not the answer. In most cases, helping others causes our problems to indirectly dissolve and answer themselves without the need to work on them directly. Logically speaking, this doesn't make sense.

Unconditional Giving Is Sometimes Inconvenient

I am usually asked to give when it is inconvenient for me—for example, when giving requires me to change my plans, take some risk, or make some sacrifice. It always seems to be when I'm hungry, or when I'm tired, or when I'm in a bad mood, or when I've worked all day and finally gotten a break that I get that phone call, asking for help. I see that as a test and a challenge, and I sometimes laugh when it happens, because, deep down below my mood of irritation, I know there are no coincidences—that timing is always perfect. The universe does not operate just to fit my schedule.

At such times, my goal is to say yes even when my self-talk says, "Don't do this." Then I start coming up with reasons not to do it. Don't listen to those thoughts, because they are just lies thrown at you by your selfish instincts, which say, "You don't have enough time. You're too tired to do it. Someone else will do it."

Step up when duty calls. That means when you're tired and don't feel like it, and it interferes with your plans. The challenge is to ignore those thoughts, and provide help regardless of your mood.

If you only help when you feel like it, or when it is convenient, or when it fits in with your schedule, you will never help anyone. The commitment I'm recommending is that whenever you are asked to help, do it regardless of how you feel in the moment. If all your giving were based on convenience, that would make it conditional, not unconditional.

Helping a Stranger Who Asks

One day, as I was just leaving a restaurant to head back to my car, an older gentleman came up and asked me, "You wouldn't happen to be going by the hospital, would you?"

That was an odd question, but I didn't even think about it. Immediately, I just said, "Yes," without any pause or hesitation at all. I didn't even give myself a chance to go, "Well…, sorry, I need to go do something right now," or give him some other BS story. I just said, "Absolutely. Where do you need to go?" It turned out that he was an older man with no transportation. He didn't ask me for money. He just needed a ride. I enjoyed meeting him, and we had a meaningful conversation on the way.

Helping Those Who Don't Give in Return

Some of us get to practice this kind of unconditional, unreciprocal, one-way giving with our children, dependent family members, or parents we're taking care of in their old age. Those we help may be mostly thinking of their own needs, wants, and demands without considering ours. Such situations give us an opportunity to practice patience, kindness, and tolerance. In some of the most challenging moments that I was helping others, I've asked myself, *If the roles were reversed, how would I want to be treated?*

HALT!

Ever heard of "HALT"? It is an acronym used in recovery programs to mean that when one is *h*ungry, *a*ngry, *l*onely, or *t*ired, it is time to stop, take care of those needs, and then proceed. When those needs are not properly taken care of, they can cause increased levels of stress hormones and bad moods, which make it difficult to be of service by giving to others.

Keep Giving Consistently, Regardless of Your Circumstances

Our challenge is to start and maintain giving unconditionally, consistently over time, regardless of our circumstances. I'm talking about consistently being an unconditional giver despite the moods we're in, despite the challenges and the various stressors that come up daily, despite being sick, despite something bad happening to a loved one, despite financial circumstances, and despite being in physical pain.

Say "Yes" to Giving Opportunities

Help others when they need it—not only when it is convenient for you or you are in the mood. When someone needs help, the timing is rarely perfect for the giver. Everything in life happens for reasons that we cannot always understand logically. There are no mistakes. Rather, there is a continual intelligent organization of circumstances that guides us from our hearts toward an outcome that benefits the greater good. Our selfish free-will choices based on instincts are constantly throwing wrenches into the plan. But the Spirit of One is constantly adjusting and updating its subtle guidance in favor of general outcomes that benefit the greater good.

Hindsight is always 20/20. After some time passes, and we examine the past, we can usually piece together the "why" that makes sense. One common explanation is, "That had to happen in order for this other thing to happen." But a more accurate explanation would be, "After everything that *does happen*, regardless of whether from a free-will choice or accident, an overall intelligence is guiding all of our hearts in ways that benefit the greater good." If someone is put in front of you who needs help, there is a reason for the timing, and why it's you who is presented with the opportunity. There are no coincidences. Through our heart, the Great Spirit is always guiding us when our free will allows it. Anyone who comes in front of me in need is put there for a reason—for me to give help. There are no coincidences. This is related to the interconnected intelligence that is continually orchestrating all life as one, always working to balance, guide, and benefit the whole—despite our individual free will choices.

"I Will Help, But Only If I Get Something Out of It"

The needy person provides an opportunity for me to give unconditionally. But such opportunities are not always perfect. The ideal opportunity would be like a beautiful single woman needing help changing a flat tire, and it just so happens that I pass by at that exact moment, without some other guy pulling over, interrupting my helping her. Oh, but shoot! There is the sex motive. My helping her is conditional. Oops.

Or I encounter a guy in a desert who needs help changing his flat tire, so I decide to stop and help because I remember the story of the guy who did just that, and it turned out to be Howard Hughes, who appeared poor, but who later rewarded the guy with a huge chunk of money! Hmmm, so I help somebody who looks poor because he might really be rich and give me some money or some other opportunity later? There's the money motive. Oops. So, I help only if *I* might benefit? Conditional giving, conditional helping, right? That's our instinct. It's natural. It's our default mode.

Will we choose to help someone who is disabled, who might be repulsive, confused, foul smelling, or hard to understand and rambling? Will we help that person, since he apparently has nothing to give us back in return? It is not always comfortable, or convenient, or desirable when the opportunity to give unconditionally arises. It is a choice we make in the moment—and it's not one we usually *want* to make.

Are All Your Interactions with People Conditional?

Are our interactions with other people, including friends, family, and strangers, based on a trade, a give-and-get? Are they all transactional, as if we are doing something *for* them to get something back *from* them? How about giving someone something for nothing in return? Do you ever do that? Are you willing to do that?

Chapter 8:
Setting Limits on Giving

Giving Money

In my experiences with giving money to various people who have asked me for help, I have noticed a trend. Many of the people I helped financially came back later, again and again, to ask for more—until I set a limit. I have learned that limits need to be set with people about giving them money. Otherwise, they usually will always ask for more, and some will attempt to make you their single source for money. You can help them temporarily, but in the long run they need to learn how to support themselves financially. I don't like having to say no. But I have learned that giving money to people usually ends up with my having to set limits.

At a Starbucks one day, I met a man around my own age who appeared to be struggling financially, but I saw no indication that he was addicted to drugs or alcohol, so I decided to give him some money without him asking. To stay in touch, we traded phone numbers. A week later, he called me to ask for more money, so he could take his dog to the vet. Without hesitation, I gave him more. A week later, he called to ask for more money, so he could go on a trip in his motorhome to visit his son, who lived three hours away. He said he needed money for gas to get there. I gave him money a third time. After another week, he called to say that he was out of town and needed money for the fourth time.

Here was the test. I didn't want to become his single source of money, so I knew I had to set a boundary. But when I told him that I wasn't going to send him money right away, he immediately became angry. He started saying things to try to manipulate me by shaming me. I was shocked when he started calling me names and said some horrible things to me. It was really disturbing to experience this from someone whom I had recently helped so much. He was attacking me for setting boundaries.

After I set those boundaries, he sent me some mean text messages. I replied with, "Love you, brother. Wish you the best." I hope that at some point he thought about his behavior and reflected on why he treated me the way he did. He had no reason to blame or hate me for anything. I didn't respond to him in any negative way. I simply gave to him, generously and unconditionally. And since I wasn't negative to him, he cannot blame me for his abusive attempts to force me to give more. Sometimes, you have to set boundaries, and then cut ties.

Some people are like children who become upset when they don't get what they want, so they lash out in abusive ways that may have worked with others in their past. They try to force others to give through guilt, shame, or even threats. With that insight, I could have justified that helping others financially is a lost cause. True, some people are ungrateful, selfish, and self-centered, and helping them may require great patience and tolerance. I would prefer it if people I helped were grateful, didn't expect more later, and showed appreciation—but that would be conditional giving.

Everyone is on a different level of self-centeredness and ignorance of the truth. To resent a person because of how much I have given him or her, and how I think I should be treated for it, means that I'm making the giving conditional. The sad truth is, if allowed to, some people will take everything I have, with no consideration at all for me and my circumstances. But I don't regret my giving. To the best of my ability, I give unconditionally, without basing it on the recipient's future behavior toward me. Nevertheless, maintaining unconditional giving can be challenging at times, and setting boundaries is necessary.

Delaying an Answer to a Financial Request

When you are asked for money, your first instinct is probably to say no. But you may not want to answer immediately, so take some time to ponder the request. Check your instincts against your heart. When you are asked for money, it is fine to take some time before making a decision. You can say, "Let me think about it, and I'll get back to you." Then you may figure out a way to help that doesn't involve money, or perhaps you can suggest how the person can get financial assistance from another source. In the end, it is totally acceptable to say no, but when you are in doubt, it is best to lean toward generosity.

Drug Addiction Increases Selfishness

Alcohol, narcotics, methamphetamines, and cocaine use frequently cause people to get addicted in a short period of time and have difficulty quitting. Then, once they are addicted, the mental and physical suffering required to stop motivate them to continue using.

The more that people use drugs like these, the more self-centered and selfish they usually become. Then the pain and suffering caused by their growing selfishness and hurting of others usually isolate them. What commonly makes people stop using these drugs are legal troubles, rejection from others, failing health—or death.

Sometimes Not Helping Others Financially Helps Them

Do not enable drug addicts by giving them money to feed their addiction. They need to have pain and consequences to get sober and stay sober. Helping addicted people financially actually hurts them by allowing them to continue to hurt themselves and everyone around them. The way to help them is by assisting them to get into detox and treatment.

A younger male friend whom I have known for over ten years started using heroin and meth. His mom reached out to me for support in helping him. That process required patience, tolerance, and sacrifice on my part, and it wasn't fun.

But I wanted to help him to survive, and get back to a place where he could give to others again. So, I was there for him when he needed it—on his schedule, not mine. I was available with my time without supporting him financially. His life was on the line. On short notice, he called me and asked me to pick him up to bring him to detox. I went by his place to pick him up, but by that time, his high had worn off, so he wouldn't go because he started looking for drugs to treat his withdrawal from opioids. When he couldn't decide to help himself, I left. I had done what I could. But ultimately, it was him passing out in his car at an intersection, getting arrested, and going to jail that got him to detox.

A year later, my young friend is sober and doing well again. Once more, he is giving back to others.

Chapter 9:
Trust

We Trust Givers

We have all had our trust broken. It hurts, saddens us, makes us fearful, and causes us to isolate ourselves from people, to the point that we interact and share less because we don't want to take the chance of getting hurt again. From experience, we learn how to filter out the people we cannot trust. We were created with instincts in order to survive by questioning the intent of others to protect ourselves. Instincts and time have trained us to judge everyone with fear and doubt.

On the other hand, we earn trust from others by giving our best self to them consistently over time, and by being reliable and dependable. I am trusted because I am trustworthy. If I break that trust, it takes a long time, if ever, to gain it back.

When Losing Trust in Others Is "Wising Up"

We have all known or watched people pretend to give unconditionally, but then later it is revealed that they had a conditional motive with an expectation of getting sex or money in return for their giving. Those motives are part of human nature. Everyone has them to various degrees. So, how can we trust that anyone gives unconditionally? Is anyone capable of unconditional giving with *no* return motive or expectation? We have all been tricked and lied to, so we wonder if unconditional giving by others is even possible. Some people think that if others have not turned cold-hearted and hard-hearted by now, it just means that they are naïve and have not yet learned. That is how many people feel. So, in a world where we need to be more and more on guard, how do we become innocent like children again after we are hurt? Becoming open to trusting is possible, but it takes time.

You're being nice to me, someone thinks. *That must mean you want something from me. You must be trying to trick me or hurt me.*

It's sad that most of us have lost trust in each other, believing that unconditional giving is impossible. We can each work to repair that negative belief by being an example for others to see that genuine unconditional giving is possible.

What the world needs is enough people to actually become unconditional givers, showing others through their example that unconditional giving is possible. We all know that building trust, like earning financial credit, takes time, and that lost trust is hard to get back. Throughout our lives, we have experienced being hurt by the selfish motives of others. We have been shaped through experience to believe that true love and true unconditional giving are not real. We have wanted to believe otherwise, but many of us have given up. Building trust in others and believing that others are capable of unconditional giving is not an overnight process. It is not a switch that we can simply flip—not when there is so much negative history.

Most people in the world are like scared, abused animals,

who need time to thaw out. It takes time for us to develop trust again once it is lost. But with witnessing and experiencing enough examples of real unconditional giving over time, it can be done. There is hope.

Healing Takes Time and Patience

Until enough people start trusting and giving unconditionally, on a wide-scale basis, many of us will be like the two cats I volunteered to keep for someone who became homeless due to a narcotic problem. The cats had been neglected and were scared. When I first got them, they didn't trust me, so I needed to be patient with them. I had to go slowly when approaching to pet them, to gain their trust over time. I talked to them in a soft voice, so they felt safe. It takes time to heal and to trust again, but it is possible with kindness, patience, and love.

Trusting That Unconditional Giving Is Possible Allows Others to Practice It

Some people have difficulty receiving from others. Why? Because they have lost trust that others can give to them unconditionally, and they don't want to owe anyone in the future, so they don't allow it. They don't trust that the giver's intentions are unconditional. But by not trusting that another is capable of unconditional giving, they don't allow the other the opportunity to give unconditionally. They don't believe that it's possible to give without motives. They suspect that anyone giving to them without terms laid out up front will have strings attached, a future expectation of sex, money, or some other future favor.

Do Not Convert Unconditional Giving to Conditional Giving

Sadly, there is not a lot of pure, unconditional giving in this world—but we can change that. Be an example of an unconditional giver to teach others that it is possible. Unfortunately, unconditional giving can be converted by us later to conditional, strings-attached giving by calling in a favor to someone we helped in the past. It is not appropriate to expect someone to pay us back if we claimed to have given unconditionally in the first place.

If an individual converts unconditional giving to conditional, that teaches others to believe that unconditional giving does not really exist. We teach others by our example. People need to witness examples of sustained unconditional giving over time to believe that it is possible, and eventually to become unconditional givers themselves.

Let's say that you decide to give someone money unconditionally. If you expect to get the money back at some point in the future, then the giving becomes conditional. To give someone money unconditionally means that you don't resent her (or him) when she has an opportunity to do something for you in the future and doesn't. Or you ask her to help you, and she declines. Will you resent her? Your instincts will tell you to. You will think that she owes you. But if you do, then you have converted an unconditional gift to a conditional one. You can justify being a victim and think about how this person should act another way because of what you did for her in the past. But the goal is to keep unconditional giving permanently unconditional. That means you are not owed anything, in any way, ever, by those to whom you give gifts.

Chapter 10:
Relationships

"I Can't Love You Until I Love Myself"

You have probably heard the saying, "You have to love your-self before you can love anyone else." Does that mean that you need to be happy and fulfilled by yourself before you can have a meaningful intimate relationship? Yes, both partners must respect and admire themselves, which comes from being of service and giving to others. You feel love and appreciation for yourself by treating others well.

Stress Is the Test for Every Relationship

The beginnings of romantic relationships are usually great, because everyone is putting on an act, showing only how nice and giving he or she can be, while hiding their selfishness. But it is only a performance. We pretend to be givers, rather than takers, for as long as we can. That is because most people are attracted to unconditional givers.

When we start dating someone new, we fantasize that he or she is completely unselfish and unconditionally loving. But even-tually, some stressful situation destroys the fantasy, exposing the other person's true selfish nature. We are always disappointed or even shocked when the other person's selfishness is revealed.

It is easy to give at the beginning of a relationship, when it is new and exciting. Everyone knows how to fake it for a month or more. But it is not easy to be loving and giving when stressful situations arise, such as jealousy, the loss of health, the loss of a job, or the death of a loved one. Stress tests the relationship.

But whenever that day comes, some deep level of trust is broken, and illusions are shattered. Sometimes a person can turn around 180 degrees by doing something completely unexpected, such as saying something unkind or mean.

Then you think, *Did you really just say that?*

Now she (or he) is not being loving the way you have always expected her to be. You may think, *Wow! I thought you were able to give more when you're under stress, and you can't. That's disappointing. Now I don't like you as much.*

Somewhere inside, a door closes and a wall is built. Then you may decide to stay in the relationship only for dependence, familiarity, or the fear of loneliness.

Whenever two people eventually face stress together as a couple, that brings their individual levels of selfishness out into the open, testing how loving and giving each party really is underneath the "giving" act in the beginning. It is in difficult circumstances that one can see how well romantic partners can give to each other unconditionally.

The Current Trend Is to Make No Commitments

Many people live for short term gratification. If something feels good now, they think, *Do it.* We live in a disposable society concerning stuff and relationships. Don't bother fixing something broken or challenging, just throw it away and get a new one. Divorce and split parenthood are the new normal. We want instant gratification. We want a fix. We want something new and different after the excitement fades and stress ruins everything. This cycle repeats over and over. We are becoming more independent, isolated, and self-centered. Not an equation for happiness.

Communicating Your Needs

What do you want? Have you told your partner exactly what you want? Have you given her an opportunity to give it to you, instead of just wishing she would read your mind? Then you become angry with her in a passive-aggressive way. Communicate what you want specifically, while remembering that the relationship is not about what you want all the time; it's about giving your partner what she wants, too. In the best relationships, both parties give to each other.

Saying "I Love You"

Saying "I love you" sometimes has strings attached. When my mom told me she loved me, I knew it was unconditional. There was nothing I could do that would cause her *not* to love me. But with my dad, it felt like his "love" was connected to my performance in school or work, which made me feel it was conditional—although, deep down, I knew he would love me, no matter what I did. Parents usually have a built-in unconditional love for their children, regardless of their behavior, and that works both ways. But of course there are exceptions.

In most intimate relationships, the partners usually love each other so long as they both provide sex and/or money to the other. If one side in an intimate partnership stops maintaining his or her role, the "love" usually fades, and then goes away completely. For example, when a man who provides financial security in a heterosexual relationship suddenly becomes unable to provide that security, his partner's "love" may decrease or cease. Unconditional love, on the other hand, is not based on circumstances.

"I love you unconditionally" means that I want you to be as happy as you can be, and I want the best for you, regardless of what I "get" from you. It is not based on me getting what I want from you or on you loving me first. Unconditional love is not based on another deserving our love because of how she has treated us.

Do you ever say "I love you" to a stranger who hasn't done anything for you? Usually not. We usually say "I love you" to others who have loved us. Sometimes we say it to people we wish we were loved by. But usually we mean it the most when we say it to others who have supported our happiness and well-being unconditionally. It is natural to love people who have loved us. If you give love, you get love. Once again, you get what you give.

On the other hand, it is difficult to love others who do not love us back.

Real Love Is the Most Valuable Thing in Life

Iggy Pop once said, while being interviewed by Anthony Bourdain, "The most valuable thing in life is being loved, and appreciating those that are giving that to me."

Chapter 11:
What Are You Teaching Others?

Example is not the main thing in influencing others. It is the only thing.

—Albert Schweitzer

We Are Always Teaching Each Other by Example

By our example, we are all constantly teaching each other how to act, how to treat others, what to say, what to like, and what not to like. What are *you* teaching others?

We all mimic each other. What are you doing for others to see? What are you teaching them to mimic? You should be aware of this responsibility because the world is learning from you. You are a part of shaping it. Are you angry, impatient, or a loose cannon? Or are you loving, forgiving, and patient? What do you want others to do when they are in your presence? How do you want them to act toward you? Because inevitably you are either a good teacher or a bad one.

We can especially see the importance of our example through our children and everyone else who is close to us. Even one little smile at a stranger can turn into hundreds of smiles to others in the future. Our influence on people with whom we make contact ripples out and influences the entire world. We all share a responsibility for our future experiences here. Are you part of the solution, or part of the problem?

Reacting to Anger

It is not easy to have a positive reaction, or no reaction at all, to someone who is angry at us or unkind to us. Instinctively, we want to reflect the anger or unkindness back—thinking, *They're asking for it!* What you give is what you get, right?

But don't we want to make others look at their destructive and negative behavior, so they will reflect on how they are acting and not blame us for their behavior? If we don't react negatively to their negativity, or don't react at all, subconsciously they may feel foolish about their behavior and reflect on what they said or did. We are giving them a chance to look at their poor behavior. But if we react negatively to their negativity, we are actually permitting them to justify what they said or did, and they will continue on with their negative behavior. In fact, they may even blame *us* for their poor reaction in the first place.

Most people react to others in like kind, because that's the instinctual reaction, but it only gives bad actors the ability to blame others for how they act. If we don't react negatively, or if we don't react at all, it's like holding up a mirror for them to look at themselves. This may sound like Yoda-level stuff, but our positive reaction or nonreaction will plant a powerful seed in the subconscious of the offender, teaching through example.

I have noticed that when people are rude to me, and I am patient and kind back to them, they usually end up feeling bad about what they said, and apologize. This is true whether they are rude to me on the phone, in an e-mail, or in person.

80

Reacting with kindness to another's anger is not something that I find easy to do, and I can't always do it. In fact, at times it's one of my most difficult challenges. The goal is progress rather than perfection.

In dealing with an angry person who is only saying things to hurt you and get an emotional response from you, the goal is to give back love and not react with negativity, either with spoken or written words. The goal is to cool down before reacting. When you feel angry and want to react with anger, don't react immediately. The goal is to pause and not immediately respond with an emotional reaction. Restrain yourself. Wait.

You will almost always regret reacting to anger from others with anger of your own. Not reacting to anger with anger is the goal. Your ultimate goal is to react with love, kindness, and forgiveness to others' anger. People who provide examples of this achievement are my heroes.

But it is hard not to respond to negativity with negativity. It is a challenge, because naturally we want to react, and even fight. But it is always best to hold your tongue and not react. Don't send the e-mail. Don't make the phone call. This is one of the most valuable lessons I have ever learned. Every time I have not said something that I really wanted to say in the heat of the moment, I have always been glad later. On the other hand, every time I did act immediately, I always regretted it later. Words cannot be unsaid or unwritten. People can always forgive, but they will never forget.

Another option for responding to someone else's negativity is to postpone your reaction by saying something like, "We need to talk about this later," and then you leave. A last resort could be not saying anything and leaving before you react.

When we respond to anger with kindness, we are teaching others how to act by example.

Who Are Your Heroes and Why?

Mainstream heroes are people who became rich or famous through some kind of talent—whether in sports, music, literature, entertainment, art, science, academia, or business.

But beyond the fame and fortune, what kind of people are they? That is what really matters. What are they giving to others besides a display of ego? We like people who help others when they become rich or famous. We like them to be humble, generous, and kind. But we don't like people who obtain fame or fortune and then just show off, live selfishly, and brag about their lifestyle and their material possessions.

People who proudly display self-centered excess are not good role models. Rich or famous people who show off their money and success, or glorify their sexual promiscuity, only teach others to strive for the same. They are only glorifying selfish instincts. Others then reflect their ignorant lessons.

Influencing and fostering a desire in others to be selfish "heroes" is not admirable. Such behavior influences others to perpetuate more pain and suffering in the world. Do we need more selfish show-offs in the world? People who are in the public spotlight have a huge responsibility, since they have a powerful influence on the masses. Do they model service to self, or service to others? Are they takers or givers?

The examples and lessons we get from the media, including popular culture, mostly glorify sex, money, and total self-centeredness.

What do the media teach and promote? Division or unity? What if the media primarily focused on stories about people helping others, being kind, being loving, being humble, and being generous? That would go a long way toward healing the world. On the other hand, I know that sex sells, and fights are entertaining. We are all hooked on seeing others' faults revealed and people getting exposed for something. Media producers have a tremendous power and responsibility with the content they provide, since it influences, teaches, and provides examples for society to mimic.

I appreciate and admire people who are kind and give to others, regardless of their mood, circumstances, or position in society. My heroes are the people who are the best examples of being unconditionally giving and of service to others. My heroes are the achievers in the giving department.

Givers Are Our Favorites

Our favorite people are the best givers. Some do it despite not having a lot to give. Next are the givers who have a lot of money and give generously; we like them, too. We like generous people. We don't like selfish people, whether they are rich or poor.

If you think about the people you really like, they are all great examples of givers. They make others feel good. They are nice, kind, generous people. They are good listeners. They care. They give us their time. They are always there when we need them. They teach us how to give by giving. They want to bring us up, not down. They provide us the examples we need in this life. Those are the people we like the most.

The Full Cycle of Human Life

Think about your parents. How did they give to you? What have you given to them? Throughout time in the life cycle, the roles in parent-child relationships change. In fact, they often reverse. Childhood, midlife, and old age are very different. In the beginning, the parents do all the giving. They give patience, tolerance, and care, with little return in kind from their children.

In the middle of life, the relationship between parents and children becomes more equal in giving and taking. Finally, at the end of the life cycle, the children are generally the ones who provide and care for the parents, so that the roles become completely reversed. Then the children are challenged to have patience, be tolerant, and take care of the parents as they become older.

Attention Is the Most Important Thing I Can Give My Child

Giving attention to my child is the most important thing I can do as a parent. When my child is bad or acting out, it is usually because she wants or needs my attention. She will take good or bad attention. She doesn't care—she just wants my attention.

Am I mostly giving her good attention or bad attention? Am I patient, kind, and tolerant? She provides me with opportunities to learn and practice those traits. She is my greatest teacher. And I am hers. What am I teaching her to be? A giver, I hope—a patient, kind, loving giver. But I also sometimes set limits and boundaries that make her temporarily angry. I can't always please her or reward her for everything, or else she wouldn't learn. Either *I* teach her, or the world will.

Sometimes I expect my daughter to know things just because

I know them. I momentarily forget that she has a lot to learn. Sometimes I catch myself being impatient. But part of my job as a parent is to explain things patiently.

We become the company we keep. My daughter is becoming the people she spends time with, which includes me. I see her developing personality traits that mimic me, her mom, and other kids. Everyone is teaching her. But her mom and I have the biggest impact. How I treat her is how she will treat others in this life, and expect to be treated.

Down Syndrome Teachers

Have you ever noticed that people with Down syndrome always seem to be happy? They are incredible examples and teachers for us. Why? Because they are not motivated by money. They are generally unselfish and truly care for others around them. They have maintained an innocence that most people lose. I automatically feel love for them, and make a point of smiling and waving at them whenever I see them. They never think that's "weird" or question my motives. They always smile and wave back.

Dog and Cat Teachers

Dogs give us love freely, and usually we don't have to earn it. With little or no effort on our part, dogs will give us love and happy energy. Just our presence makes them happy. However, with cats, it's a different story. Usually, we need to give them love for some time, and then gradually they will start to give us love back. But only when they *decide* to love us back. And it's usually not consistent or available every time we want it. We usually have to put more effort into earning affection from a cat than from a dog. Cats teach us relationship-building skills that involve the effort of giving to get. Most dogs give regardless, whether we deserve it or not. Cats are more in the delayed gratification category, requiring more patience. Dogs usually fall into the instant gratification category—that is, with little effort, we usually get the immediate love and attention we crave.

Some people don't like cats, but almost everyone likes dogs. Why? Because dogs are more consistent givers. Every time you come home, they are so glad to see you! So happy that you are there! They respond so easily and positively, without much effort or sweet talk. In return, we love them back. They are giving love to get love. Dogs are very important teachers for us. They help us learn these lessons. Even if we abuse them, they still love us, and they will also show us forgiveness. Dogs don't hold grudges. They always forgive and teach us that valuable lesson through example. Whether we are aware of it or not, dogs are actually teaching us how to treat other people.

Attractive Qualities

Kindness, love, tolerance, patience, humility, and generosity are attractive qualities. Despite physical appearance, we are drawn to people with those qualities—just as we are repelled by people who are unkind, unloving, intolerant, impatient, arrogant, and greedy. How attractive are *you?*

Every Choice Matters

A friend of mine was driving with a handicapped parking pass hanging from his rearview mirror, when he pulled up to a store we were going into. There was only one handicap spot available, and he took it.

As he started to get out, I looked at him and said, "Whoa, wait! Are you handicapped?"

He said, "Nah, that was for my mom."

"Well, your mom passed away a year ago," I said. "So, what's this still doing up here? We need to park somewhere else. Somebody else needs this spot…, somebody who's handicapped."

He replied, "Man, thanks. You're right."

Every choice and every action you take matters.

Following My Heart, Not My Head

I was recently eating lunch at a small restaurant, when a man walked by my table, dropped a pack of gum down, and walked away. Then I saw that he was going table to table, doing the same thing. A message was taped to the pack of the gum, which read, "Hello, I am deaf. I am selling this gum to support my family. Will you buy this one for $2 if you wish? Tips lucky. Thank you."

Without hesitation, and not listening to any selfish thoughts, I slipped a hundred-dollar bill under the pack of gum, and couldn't wait for him to come pick it up.

When he finally came back around, he saw the cash and mouthed, "Thank you."

I was sitting, and he was standing, so I put my hand out to shake his, but didn't let go. Instead, I pulled him a little closer, looked into his eyes, and mouthed the words "I love you."

He smiled, showing a mouth full of rotten teeth. His eyes welled up with tears.

Chapter 12:
Ideas for Giving

The Most Valuable Thing I Can Give
to Others Is My Attention

Dale Carnegie's bestselling book, *How to Win Friends and Influence People*, reveals that listening to others is how we get them to like us. Just listen to them with interest. We like people who listen to us. According to Carnegie, we don't have to tell others anything about ourselves for them to like us. We just have to be good listeners by making continual eye contact, smiling, nodding, validating them as they speak with "right" and "yes," and asking questions about what they are saying to keep them talking about themselves. Even if you have just met them, and they haven't learned anything at all about you, after you listen to them intently for a short time, they will feel that they like you. People want to be heard and validated, more than they want to hear and learn about us. People yearn to connect, for others to know them. Good listening provides that.

Here is a suggestion for practicing good listening: Once again, call a friend, ask how he is doing, and then listen without interrupting. While listening, give him feedback and ask questions based on what he has talked about. Keep the conversation on his topic.

Being a good listener takes a lot of patience, and it is hard to listen without interrupting. Sometimes, I find that I want to do most of the talking, so not interrupting is challenging. It can be difficult to listen to all of what the other person is saying without half-listening, or half-thinking about your response, and then interrupting with it before he finishes his thoughts or story. Before I respond, I try to let him keep going until there is an obvious pause, when he has said all he needs to. It is not easy to be a good listener. We all want to talk and be heard.

I also notice that I want to "solve a problem," or "teach," and then move on in the conversation. The longer I can listen without interrupting, however, the more "giving" my listening is. This is all that many counselors do: they encourage their patients to talk, then repeat back what they hear to indicate they are listening, and then they continue to ask questions in order to fully understand a problem before they give feedback.

But if I am impatient, and I don't want to wait for the full story or all the information, I will interrupt and start giving my premature analysis, and my own desire to be heard.

When you are listening to someone who is expressing emotional pain, if you haven't had the same experience, *don't* say, "I know how you feel," because you don't. It's only okay to say, "I know how you feel" if you have had the same pain or experience. Otherwise, just validate his sharing of a painful event or experience by saying something factual, such as, "That must make you feel sad," or "That sounds very painful." You could also say, "I can't imagine how hard this has been for you." That shows that you recognize and acknowledge his pain and that you are listening.

In general, listening is like giving, whereas talking is like taking. So the goal is to give more, to listen more, and talk less—or talk less about ourselves, which can be challenging.

Sometimes there are people who start talking and won't stop, as if they want to hold us hostage to listening to them. They blab on and on, never getting to any point, and you can hardly take ten more seconds of their talking. But realize that no one else wants to listen to them, either. People who do this are extremely lonely and desperate to connect with others, but their behavior pushes others away. It is too intense, so it becomes a form of self-sabotage.

Since I know this, I try to give such people my full attention and patience for as long as I can tolerate it. I do my best to listen, thinking, *I'm here for you, and what you're telling me is the most important thing I've ever heard.* I do my best not to display body language such as fidgeting or looking away as if I'm about to run, to give them at least a few moments of real listening. It's not easy to do, and some people should have a pause or stop button on their forehead. But their behavior provides good opportunities to practice giving.

Think of any friend you haven't spoken to in a while, and call him (or her) right now and ask how he's doing. Then just listen. Don't talk about yourself at all, and don't talk about your life—even if he asks. Redirect back to him and keep the focus on him and his life. It's hard not to talk about yourself, but once you hear what he's got to say, come up with some ideas for how you can help him and give to him concerning his issues or problems. Ask him the right questions to pull his answer out of him, such as, "What do you need right now? How can I help you with that? What can I do for you today? When can I help you?" Figure out how he could use your help right now. It may just be your listening to him is all he really needs.

Giving Compliments

Compliments are another way of giving. I walked up to my daughter one day as she was brushing her hair and looking at herself in the mirror. I paused behind her, looking at her reflection, and said, "My beautiful, special child, who doesn't even know how beautiful and special she is." Then I just smiled at her. I could see that it made her feel good inside. Are you planting beautiful, positive, life-affirming thoughts in your children and the other people you are in contact with?

To people you care about, you can say, "I need to tell you something." Then genuinely tell them specifically what you admire and appreciate most about them.

One great way to compliment people close to you is to exaggerate a compliment. So, I just said to my daughter as we were walking out the door to take her to school, "Come on, my sweet, beautiful child, who's so smart and special, with a special heart, who's so sweet and giving to me and others. My little love." After I said all that, she started skipping around and smiling at me. It was priceless!

Text Others Meaningful Words from Your Heart

Think of someone important to you and then text her a message, saying what she means to you. For example, "Hey, I was just thinking about you—and that you mean a lot to me, and I'm grateful you're in my life."

We don't do that enough. Or just say, "I love you. I was thinking about you." Or, "Do you know how special you are to me? You mean a lot to me, and my life is so much better because you are in it. I just wanted to let you know that."

It's incredible how powerful positive words and feedback can be to other people. It will mean more to them than you think it does.

Free Compliments—A Great Idea

I was at a large public fair recently, when I saw a guy sitting in a chair with a sign around his neck that read, "Free Compliments."

Wow! What an idea and a conversation starter! He's giving compliments to get compliments in real time. I watched him complimenting people as they walked by, and they stopped to do the same in return. Everyone was smiling. I admired his idea, and appreciated his example.

Smile Often

I love it when someone gives me a big smile for no reason. Is it okay to smile at other people for no reason with sustained eye contact? Isn't that risky? Won't they think I have selfish motives or perverted intentions? Not if I do it from the heart, while silently saying, "I love you." People can know without any words spoken that your smile is simply a gift, with no selfish intentions.

Muster the courage to be the first to smile, to be a leader, to be a teacher, and create a ripple of good feelings. Make eye contact with others and smile as often as you can remember. It is giving without saying a word. It is asking strangers to trust that your intention is pure, and they can receive it without fear.

With practice, you get more smiles back, and fewer awkward glances away. I have memories of people who decided to give me a big smile and eye contact for no reason I could think of at the moment, but that made me feel good nevertheless. Smiling is something free and simple that we can give to others.

It Feels Good to Give Others Opportunities to Give

One time, I went into a gas station to get something to drink. At checkout, I gave the clerk $20, and the change was just under $18. Without anyone else hearing me, I leaned in and said, "I want you to keep the change, and then pay for everybody coming behind me until the money's used up."

He said, "Uhm…, okay."

I walked out, feeling good that I had just given a gift to the people in line behind me, and also that I had given the clerk the opportunity to be a part of giving, which was going to make him feel good, too. I gave him the ability to give. Giving directly feels good, but giving indirectly also feels good.

Always Having to "Get the Deal" Is Not Very Giving

When you are buying something or negotiating with others, do you always need to bargain down the price and get the better deal? If you do, that is not giving. How about paying full price, and giving the other party the better deal?

My suggestion is to give more than the other party expects in every transaction. For example, tip double what you normally do. When I've done that, sometimes the waiter will ask, "Are you sure?" And I'll say, "Yes, of course I'm sure." I've had people ask, "Why are you doing this? I can't accept this." And I will reply, "Why not?"

Don't be stingy, unless you want the world to be that way with you. It's a cycle. What you are giving out, and how you are giving it, comes back to you in kind over time. It may not come the next day or the next week. It may come years down the road. But it will come. It has happened to me. How you are treating others now will determine the quality of your future.

Traffic Provides Opportunities to Practice Giving

When people are in traffic, they commonly express anger and impatience. It resembles how people act like fools behind their computers on social media. We say and do things while we are driving or are on social media that we normally wouldn't say or do if we were face-to-face with people. I sometimes find myself name-calling out loud while I'm driving, in ways I would never do outside the car. That will happen, for example, if someone cuts in front of me, follows too closely, or doesn't let me in and then pretends to look the other way. It can also happen if someone gives me a negative gesture when *I* commit one of those acts. So, traffic gives me multiple opportunities to practice patience and forgiveness, and not react immediately with anger.

How do we practice giving to others while driving, instead of having visible big baby anger fits? Try deciding to let someone else go ahead of you, or let someone have a parking spot that you are about to pull into. If someone is "cutting" in front of you, let them in. Give it to them, even if it's not their turn. That isn't easy, but it's a way to practice unconditional giving.

Always Be Nice to People in Service Positions

How do you treat customer service people on the phone? Like punching bags? They are not their company, and they are not responsible for making the dumb policy you are so mad about. When I talk to customer service representatives, I am always extra nice to them.

I also make it a point to be extra kind to wait staff. Don't abuse your power or position just because you can. Be nice to others regardless of their position. Always be nice to people who are serving you. That is a simple way to give.

Kindness is always the *right* choice, but not always the *easy* choice.

Listening to My Heart with a Homeless Couple

One day, while I was driving, I passed a familiar couple on a street corner. They were both in their fifties or sixties, and seemed to be arguing. The woman had short blond hair, was missing a lot of teeth, and was dressed all in black, including her cap. The man, who had grey hair in a ponytail, had a rough-and-beat-up look. I had seen them around my area for at least a year, but I had never spoken to them.

My heart said, "Stop. Pull over. Help them. Do something for them."

So, I pulled over, parked near them, and watched them from my car for a minute. All the while, I was thinking, *What can I do? I don't want to give them money. That's stupid. That will only enable them to get high and drunk. They must be addicts. What can I do to help them?*

I started coming up with all these reasons not to do anything. *Maybe*, I thought, *I'll help them tomorrow.*

But I didn't listen to that selfish chatter. I ignored it, got out of my car, walked right over to them, and waited for them to make eye contact with me. When they did, I said, "Hey, do y'all want to go get somethin' to eat?"

I hadn't planned on saying that. It just came out. Because that was simple. I could buy them something to eat, and leave. That wouldn't be hard.

The woman said, "Sure, that would be great," and the man agreed.

So, I asked where they wanted to go and waved for them to follow me back to my car.

As the woman got into the car, she said, "Denny's."

So, Denny's it was.

As we drove there, I looked at the woman and asked, "Tell me, how are you doing?"

She immediately started telling me about how she suffered from panic attacks and had anxiety problems. I could tell she was very scattered mentally. Soon I learned that she and the guy had been together for five years and been married for a year and a half.

The man was physically disabled, had health problems, and was probably an alcoholic.

To my surprise, the woman said that she had been a nurse before she developed her mental problems, and that she needed to get her life together so she would be able to "give again."

Now, what are the odds that the word *giving* would be one of the first words out of her mouth after they got in the car, and specifically, that she wanted to be in a position to give again? I briefly thought about telling them about my revelations, which had happened about a month before, but I didn't because I didn't want to get all preachy about giving. So, I just stayed in the moment, listened to both of them talk, and took them to a Denny's, where I bought them some food and did my best just to listen. That's it. It was just reaching out to some people who looked like they could use a little help at the moment with a meal and some nonjudgmental company.

Nothing Feels Better Than Giving to Others

For the last twenty years, one of my hobbies has been prepping for disaster—specifically, researching and obtaining the best supplies for survival in the event of a natural or man-made calamity. For years, I have collected all the best supplies in every category, including backpacks, tents, sleeping bags, stoves, lighting, etc., in order to at least have the ability to survive without relying on outside resources to meet the basic needs of food, shelter, and water.

I have a routine of going for breakfast to a local McDonald's, where I recently noticed a woman who appeared to be homeless, because her clothes and backpack were dirty. She would come in there just to get out of the cold and rain.

So, I decided to put a backpack together for her, filled with useful items for living outdoors. While I was doing this for her, I remembered a guy who was into camping, and decided that I wanted to set him up with some of my gear, too. I ended up packing two backpacks full to the top with all the best equipment for living outdoors. I never thought for a second about the money those things had cost me. I was operating above my instincts. All I could think about was the joy of imagining what they would feel like when I gave them these things. I would experience their joy and surprise.

The next day, I put both backpacks in the trunk of my car and headed to McDonald's. But the woman wasn't there. However, a man and woman, who appeared to be in their sixties, were sitting on the other side of the restaurant. They looked homeless, so I walked over to them, and said, "Hey, how are you doing?" Then I asked them where they were from.

The man said he was from Louisiana, and that he and his wife had come up to Seattle after the flood in New Orleans caused by Katrina, which had destroyed everything they owned. They had come to Seattle to do union work in tile and marble, but the work didn't come through as they had expected, and they didn't have anybody up here to help them.

Then the woman told me that they had slept outside the night before without proper bedding, because they didn't want to be separated in a shelter.

I still had those two loaded backpacks in my trunk, so I said, "Follow me out to my car."

Both backpacks were fully loaded with all the supplies needed to survive comfortably outdoors. There were camouflage Gore-Tex tents, high-end lightweight goose-down sleeping bags, multi-fuel stoves, titanium cup pots, high-end headlamps, extra lithium batteries, nice pocket knives, mace, nice sleeping pads, water filters, and many other goodies for living out of a backpack.

I opened my trunk and handed each of them a loaded pack.

The feeling of giving that stuff to those two people was priceless.

And, yes, I went home and packed two more backpacks to give to the people I had originally intended them for.

I Asked My Daughter, "Why Be a Giver?"

"Is it better to be a giver or a taker," I asked my daughter. "And why?"

My daughter, who was 7 at the time, responded: "A giver. You want to be a giver, so you always give back, and you get a lot of love back, and you don't get things taken from you."

Be Real

Here's a mantra for you: "I give wherever I go."

Here's another one: "Instead of asking people, 'How are you

doing?' ask them, 'How are you *really* doing?' This can be followed up with 'How can I help you today?' or 'Do you need help with anything?'"

Ask questions to find out how you can really help.

Business Giving: Give with No Catch

If a business advertises something for "free," you know there's always a catch. How many businesses give away something with no condition, action, or requirements from the consumer?

At my retail store, I give to my customers with low-margin prices and great customer service. And the customer is always right. Even if the customer is wrong, he's right. When a customer presents any problem, I listen with a smile, and I offer him something above and beyond to solve the problem—even if he is in the wrong. I do my best not to be negative in any way—not with my tone, my attitude, or my questions. I do whatever it takes to result in a positive experience. My goal is to always give more than the customer expects.

How is your business giving? How are you giving? Because, remember: the more you give to your customers, the bigger your business will grow. Word of mouth is powerful advertising. People will market for you because they want to. What does your business do that makes people go out of their way to tell others that you are giving? For any company or business model you like, I bet it's because they're giving in ways that set them apart. People like companies that give.

Here is another example of how I give to my customers. At my retail store, I fill up a couple of boxes with extra stock items worth anywhere from ten to eighty dollars each. I set the boxes on a bottom shelf in the front of the store. At any given time, I announce to all the customers in the store that they can pick out one free item from the boxes. When they see the quality of what I am giving away, they are very pleased, excited, and grateful. I love giving. Anne Frank once said, "No one has ever become poor by giving."

For a company to give away stuff with no strings attached is not only the most effective form of marketing, but it is also the least expensive for results. Remember, what you give comes back to you. And in business, that means *more* business.

Exercise = Better Mood = Better Giver

Exercise has always made me feel better. It relieves stress and gives me a good feeling mentally and an overall sense of well-being. But exercise requires continual action and effort on my part. Exercising improves my overall mood, so I'm more likely to be willing to be of service to others if presented with an opportunity to do so.

Every time I exercise, my guesstimate is that I earn at least a 50 percent increase in my positive mood for the rest of that day. If I don't exercise regularly, my stress level will build up, and I will feel irritable, moody, and depressed. For me, exercise makes a very powerful difference in my life. When I exercise, I can deal with stress because I feel relaxed and normal. When I exercise, endorphins are released into my bloodstream, which feels good. Do I want to run for thirty-five minutes? No. For the first two minutes, I am usually thinking, *This is hard. Stop!* But I keep going even though it's hard, because I know I need to do it for the mood benefits and stress relief.

To "earn" something means "to get results from effort." To exercise is to earn. The results cannot be given to me. They are earned through my effort. But effort is required. Action is required. Nobody else can do it for me. I can't pay someone to exercise for me. I can pay someone to train me, but I have to do the work part myself. I have to work for my good moods and a better body by choosing to exercise regularly.

Even when I have put off working out for a while because I was sick, when I go back, as soon as I start doing some weights and cardiovascular exercises, I begin to feel better mentally about halfway through the workout, and then for the rest of that day. So, exercise does provide immediate gratification during and after the workout, and I will sleep better that night, too.

Please see a doctor or get a trainer for specific advice before starting exercise if you are not in good shape or you are unsure about how to proceed. If you have never worked out, you will still have mental benefits from the very first day you give it a try. There will be a direct correlation between what you did, which wasn't easy when you started, and how you feel mentally afterward. And you will have earned that feeling. Your body will thank you for the hard work with good feelings and an improved mood. Then, by continuing to exercise over time, you will get the positive mental results that translate into your being a better giver. Also, the overall health and shape of your body will improve, along with your moods.

Chapter 13:
Forgiveness

Forgive **defined:**

- *To stop feeling angry or resentful toward someone for an offense, flaw, or mistake.*
- *To cancel a debt.*

Forgiving Means Giving Before It Is Deserved or Earned

To forgive means to give before that is deserved. The *for* part means "before" or "ahead of." But before or ahead of what? You give before you are paid back. You give before you get the other person's apology, or reconciliation, or even acknowledgment that what was done to you was wrong. It's *for-give*, not *after-this-happens-give*.

Never Lend Money

Never lend money to friends or family members unless you want to ensure future resentment and ruin the relationship. That has happened to me over and over again. If a borrower does not pay me back, or does not ever bring up the subject of repayment voluntarily, I start thinking about it, and get mad at the person. Also, most people who ask for loans have bad credit, so they are unlikely to pay you back. Don't lend money. If you give conditionally, you expect to be paid back. But if you give unconditionally, you do not expect to be repaid. If you lend people money, they will probably fall short in meeting your expectations on repayment, and the relationships will suffer for it.

I suggest that you release everyone currently in your debt, which will relieve the resentments, and then begin the true practice of unconditional giving. A month after my revelations in January 2018, I did that with five different people who owed me money. Before I forgave them, every time I saw them on Facebook, posting some trip they were taking or showing off something they had bought, instead of paying me back, I would feel pissed off at them all over again. So I decided to forgive them all. I texted each one with the message, "I forgive you of all the debt you owe me." That was it—short and sweet. Then I received some thank-you texts back.

Do you have any outstanding loans with people who owe you? Do you resent and hate someone because he (or she) defaulted, doesn't respond to you, and doesn't seem to care about paying you back? Call or text him right now, and say, "You're forgiven of your debt to me." If people owe you an outstanding debt, it doesn't matter if they haven't paid you, or if they've blown you off, or didn't appreciate it, or didn't return your calls, or even if they responded to you angrily or disrespectfully because you asked for repayment. If you want to be free of the turmoil in your head, practice real giving and forgive them of the debt.

Take the burden of repayment off your debtors. Give that gift to them. Yes, I'm suggesting that you do that even if they don't deserve it. Practice real forgiveness. I know it's not easy, but the best part is, you will get more relief than they will. I know that I have.

Wouldn't you want someone to do that for you? I would. Those people probably didn't feel good about not paying me back, but I did *my* part. Plus I taught them a lesson, planting a seed by my example of how I handled the situation with undeserved forgiveness. They were in the wrong for not settling an agreement they had made, but I was wrong to offer help with an expectation that I would be repaid. After forgiving the debts, I became free of my anger and resentment toward them, which was affecting *me*, not them. Going forward, I will never lend money to people again. I will give money to them, or not give it, but I will never lend it.

Asking for Forgiveness

In my retail business, sometimes a customer has a problem and gets angry and defensive. When that happens, I do my best to assume that there is a misunderstanding, so I attempt to ask questions from a calm, humble place to find a solution that makes the customer happy, even if I think he is "wrong" or has overreacted to something. Initially, I forgive him, following the rule that "the customer is always right," but then, if I decide that the fault is mine, I ask him to forgive me.

Just recently, an employee of mine had to look up the price of an item on the store computer. After hearing the price, the customer said it was too high and started to walk out. Then the employee rechecked the wholesale cost on the computer, realized he had looked at the wrong price, and called to the customer, "Hey, wait! I was wrong. The price is less." But the customer had left the store. I was in the back of the store and didn't witness any of this, but my employee came to me and quickly explained the details.

I followed the customer outside, and said, "Hey, I know we

made a mistake, but can you please forgive us?"

He replied, "Well, I don't like being lied to."

The customer said that my employee had been dishonest, and was now just trying to save the sale.

I didn't argue that point, but just said, "We made a mistake. Can you forgive us, give us a second chance?"

He paused for a moment, and then said, "Yeah, I guess it could have been a mistake and not a lie."

He quickly went from angry to friendly and forgiving. Why? Because I didn't argue right or wrong. I just humbly asked for his forgiveness. He then walked back into the store to purchase the item. I returned to the back of the store as the customer worked with the employee on the purchase. When I came out a few minutes later, I said that I wanted to throw in another item for free. Then I learned that the customer had already said to my employee that he wanted to pay over and above the listed price for the item. The vibe I felt was that he and my employee were reunited family. The key to this whole situation was that I asked for forgiveness directly, without arguing about the details. I just said, humbly and calmly, "Can you please forgive us?" and waited for his answer. People do want to forgive, and they need to forgive. Sometimes they just need to be asked humbly for their forgiveness.

Forgiveness Is Always the Solution

Staying angry and resentful prevents us from being givers in life. Forgiveness is the ultimate give—especially if the anger and resentment are justified, because then the act of forgiveness requires the ultimate unconditional give—which is difficult because it is the complete opposite of what we feel like doing.

Thumbs-Up and Smile—I Forgive You for Being an Idiot

One day, as I was driving, I had to slam on my brakes as a guy started to walk across the street right in front of me without even looking. Usually, my first reaction, which is a typical human reaction, is to think, *What are you doing, you idiot?*

But that time, I gave him a thumbs-up and smiled instead, and he smiled back. I could see him relax. He knew he had messed up. I could tell, in the back of his mind, he was thinking, *Thank you for not giving me the "What are you doing, idiot?" look.*

He deserved that look, but I didn't give it to him. Instead, I immediately forgave him and acknowledged that with my smile. Maybe the next time someone walks in front of his car without looking, he will remember what I did, and he will give that person a similar break. We are always teaching each other how to react by our actions. The world we live in is continually shaped by all of us, one choice at a time.

It Takes Courage and Humility to Apologize When We Are Wrong

It is really hard for most people to admit when they are wrong. It takes courage and humility, and I admire and respect people who have those qualities. I look up to them because they teach me by their example. Those are the people I want most to be around. Not everyone can say, "You know what? You're right, and I'm wrong. I should have said this or done that differently."

Forgive Others When They Apologize for Being Wrong

When people admit they are wrong and apologize for it, don't rub their noses in the problem, or continue to punish them for how ignorant they were. Just forgive them, because that's what we want people to do for us when we're in the same boat. That's how it works. What goes around comes around. How you treat others is how you will be treated.

There Is No Defense Against Love

Some good responses to ignorance, hate, and anger include: "I forgive you," "Bless you," and "I love you."

A wise man once told me, "There is no defense against love."

The Solution to Racism Is Forgiveness

Our own individual perspectives, life experiences, and cultures come into play when racism is concerned. People of all races can and do selfishly harm others. The human race needs to come together. Racism and reverse racism keep the cycle of hate going.

Racism and reverse racism both exist. Our experience with racism depends on where we have lived, and what races we have lived among. For the past twenty years, I have lived in Seattle, which has a highly diverse population of races and cultures. I am originally from Louisiana, where the population is much less diverse: 62 percent white, 32 percent black, and the other 6 percent other. I am white. Whites first brought blacks into the United States as slaves, which was selfish and horrible. Blacks, please forgive white people for the wrongs they did to you in the past. I know it's a big ask. But I'm asking: please forgive.

Being white in Louisiana, I experienced reverse racism from blacks—that is, I had some negative racist experiences from black people because I am white.

After high school, I attended college in Montana, where I

noticed a similar racism between whites and Native Americans. Since I hadn't grown up in Montana, I didn't have any experience with reverse racism from Native Americans, so I had compassion and empathy for them when I moved to that area. However, I soon noticed negative vibes directed toward me from some Native Americans because I am white.

Even if the side that was abused in the past has more reason to extend the hate, forgiveness is always the answer. But it's never an easy answer. It's hard to forgive when there is justified anger.

Forgiving is the only solution that helps us all to move forward. Without forgiveness, there is an open-ended "victim" card to play, based on justified resentment and anger. Forgiveness is the only answer that will work for the greater good, healing everyone. Hate breeds hate. Love breeds love.

It is time to move on and forgive. Otherwise, "what you give is what you get" becomes a vicious cycle of hate. That cycle can only be broken by forgiveness. Keeping the hate going around and around in circles is not the answer, even if our history seemingly justifies it. Promoting division and encouraging a victim mentality are not part of the solution in today's world.

When I feel hated, that makes me want to hate back. It doesn't lead me to want to forgive or have compassion for another's perspective or experience. If we give hate, we will get hate back. It's that simple. What do you want? Who will step up to be the party of real change to heal this world of racism with forgiveness? Who will forgive the haters, regardless of side or race? Who will do the heavy lifting?

Arguing is a natural behavior among humans. We encourage it. Who makes the hard choice of forgiving? The solutions are forgiveness, tolerance, and kindness from both sides. Someone needs to make the hard choice of forgiving the other. We need to come together and eliminate the division, hate, and arguing. We—you and I—need to be the first to extend a hand of forgiveness to the other. Be the first to unconditionally forgive. Be an example.

But you may say, "*They* should be the first ones to give."

No! Stop! *You* must be the first. Lead by example. Forgiving heals. It's not about what you want to give, or what your instincts want to do, which is to point your finger and argue. It is about what you *need* to do, which is to be the one to extend the hand and forgive, to start the healing. Can you forgive even though you have justified anger and hate? That is what is required to fix this world.

Stress, anger, and hate actually make the hater—not the hated—mentally and physically ill. I am suggesting that you do your best by reacting to hate with love and forgiveness. It will not be easy. In fact, it will be very difficult. But it will not be impossible. Become an example of an Expert Giver to be part of healing our world.

Martin Luther King, Jr., said, "We need to love each other, people."

Who is right or who is wrong doesn't matter. Forgiveness and love are the answer. Please be part of the solution and not part of the problem.

Homosexuality Exists by Design—Live and Let Live

Many Christians believe that homosexuality is a sin, because in the Old Testament it is called an "abomination," and a few disciples in the New Testament said it was a sin. But did Jesus say it was a sin, or wrong? No. He said nothing about the subject—at least nothing that was recorded. God does not make mistakes.

Everything on this planet has a purpose by design. Newsflash: some people are born gay, while others become gay later.

Everything on this planet, including our lives, is created by design with a connected, intelligent purpose. But much of that purpose is beyond our limited intelligence. Whether we understand the purpose, or connect the dots on the "why does this exist?" is another story. The most obvious reason that some humans are born as homosexuals is to control the size of the population. There are no mistakes here. At this point, we could use a lot more homosexuals on the planet. We should celebrate people being gay, because it helps to control the exponentially increasing population boom that is the number-one problem facing the human race. By not having children, homosexuals benefit the continuation of the human species more than straight people do.

I took a class in college called Animal Science, in which I learned that 10 percent of male sheep, the rams, are homosexual. They will only have sex with, and associate with, other rams. I guess there are a lot of "sinning" sheep out there, eh? Do those sheep need some kind of "re-education"? Did God make a mistake on that one? No. There are no mistakes. Everything here has a purpose that we may or may not yet understand, which benefits the whole.

Homosexuality has also been observed in orangutans, American bison, bats, pigeons, elephants, lions, dolphins, penguins, giraffes, swans, and many other species. Are they mistakes made by creation/evolution, or is there a reason we don't understand? Should those animals be "rehabilitated" or undergo therapy to make them "straight"? Or should they all be destroyed?

The "problem" is simply that homosexuals don't meet the standards or ideals for straight people, and there are more straight people than gay people. Homosexuality makes some straight people feel uncomfortable. But straight people, especially straight Christian people, need to deal with this issue as Jesus would have dealt with it. Would Jesus judge or condemn homosexuals? Did he? The perspective of straight people is not the only perspective on this Earth. Other sexual orientations exist and need to be accepted and tolerated. We are all so self-centered and judgmental as humans, which comes from our own perspective and preferences. We want to impose our own individual standards, preferences, and perspectives on others who are different. Whether we are gay or straight, we want others to conform to our preferences. For most of history, homosexuals have been persecuted and had to remain in hiding. Many Muslim countries still persecute homosexuals and put them to death.

As a straight male, I don't like to think about gay people having sex or kissing, and I don't want to see it, imagine it, or hear about it. It repulses me and makes me uncomfortable. Does that mean that homosexuality is wrong, that it should be prohibited by law, because I feel that way and think that way? Of course not! That's just my reaction coming from my perspective of being a straight male.

Is being straight the "ideal" because it is "natural" for the majority? No. So, should straight people judge or condemn homosexuals because they are repulsed by their behavior? No. That view denies the fact that some humans are born gay by design. If you ask gay people if they like to see or imagine straight people having sex, it repulses them, too. But their views don't count?

Homosexuals don't "choose" to be gay any more than straight people "choose" to be straight. Asking a homosexual to "choose" to go straight is no different from asking a straight person to "choose" to go gay. It's really ridiculous that this logic of "choosing" even exists in today's world. It's just ignorant, intolerant, judgmental crap. As far as Christianity goes, remember that Jesus was all about kindness, love, patience, and tolerance—*inc*lusion, not *ex*clusion.

Are gay people rubbing their grievances in straight people's faces these days? Yes, they are—in the name of correcting past injustice and judgment. It's a reaction to the fact that, for most of history, gay people have been killed, suppressed, shamed, and forced to live "in the closet." So, we're witnessing some vengeance today—a justified resentment to get back at straight people, and the Christian churches in particular, for the suffering they inflicted on the gay community for so long. Should gay people unconditionally forgive straight people, regardless of whether they are justified in their argument or in their reasons for resentment? Yes, if they want to be part of healing our world. Unconditional forgiveness is the answer. Gay people, please forgive straight people and the church for all the judgement and persecution in the past and present. Humility, forgiveness, and acceptance are required on both sides to heal this issue.

I can clearly see other reasons aside from population control that homosexuals were created as part of a design. Many gay people teach straight people important lessons by being extremely positive, loving, friendly, and generous human beings. That has been my experience. Some of the best examples of loving partnerships that I have ever seen have been gay men in long-term relationships. Straight people can learn from gay people's examples of how to be giving, loving, kind, and patient with each other in relationships. What gay people do behind closed doors is their own business. I don't understand it or desire it from my straight perspective, but I don't need to, because I wasn't created and designed that way. As a straight person, I just need to accept it, and not judge it. Gay people are not mistakes. I don't expect gay people not to be gay just to make straight people more comfortable around them.

We need to see each other as a family, regardless of whether we are straight or gay. For me to say that you should live according to my perspective would be foolish, and it's the same for the other side. Straight or gay, live and let live. Don't judge. Mind your own business! Love one another. Come together. Stop fighting. You have a choice.

Acceptance and forgiveness are the answer. There is painful history to overcome. Let's do our best to be considerate with each other. It takes humility to admit being wrong—especially if one side has been more wrong than the other throughout history. I am asking each side to forgive, but I am asking homosexuals, the more wronged party, to forgive first. I know it's a big ask and a big give. But your example of forgiveness will teach others how to forgive. Remember, forgiving is not just for you, it's for all of us, because, behind the scenes, there are no sides. It's all for One, and One for all. I forgive you, and you forgive me, because I *am* you, and you *are* me. Division and separation are an illusion, based on ignorance. Please be an example of forgiveness despite having justified hate and anger in others.

My intention for Expert Giver Groups is to help us come together regardless of sexual orientation, gender, religion, political association, or race.

Chapter 14:
What's My Purpose in Life?

Is Your Life's Purpose Expressed in Your Occupation?

While your work at the moment may not make you feel that you are serving your purpose to the fullest, you may still be acquiring skills and character traits that are necessary for more rewarding work later. Your purpose and your occupation are not always directly related. Your occupation may be more related to having an income to meet your basic needs, rather than a way of expressing your purpose in life. Even if that is the case, are you offering your personal best with whatever work you are doing at the moment? I really admire people who have a job that doesn't look like fun, but they are still performing their best, and doing it with a great attitude.

I have heard other people say, "Do what you love, and the money will follow." But all people can't do what they love. If that were the case, there would never be anyone willing to stock grocery stores, clean toilets, or dig ditches. By doing jobs that no one else wants to do, those people are giving necessary services to the rest of us.

I remember when I graduated from college with a bachelor's degree in business, I thought to myself, *What am I going to do with my life now?* I didn't have a clue.

Many people seek occupations based on how much money they can earn, not on how those occupations allow them to express their unique talents for serving others and the greater good.

I have never felt that I was expressing my true purpose or calling in life with any of the occupations I've had. When I had my revelations occur at the age of 48, I was given a clear purpose and calling in life. But so far, my purpose and calling are not part of an occupation providing a financial income.

In the past I have asked myself, *What occupations make people happy?* I saw people with occupations as artists or musicians who seemed happy, but I didn't have those talents. My instinctual drives had always steered me to think about occupations in which I could make more money, instead of those in which I could express my unique talents and abilities for the greater good. Instinctual drives for financial security powerfully influence our occupational choices.

Do you not know your purpose yet? It may be outside of an occupation. You may not feel a deeper purpose in your occupation or job. But in the meantime, just keep giving the best you can in the occupation you have. Look around for who is truly happy. How and what are they doing for work? In many cases, they don't have prestigious or glamorous jobs. But they benefit others by giving in some way, directly or indirectly. Do you want to be loved or envied? One time, a stranger left a note for me that said: "Those who will be truly happy will be those who have sought and found how they are best at serving others."

All the jobs I didn't "like" in the past were preparing me for something more rewarding later. Looking back, I can see that jobs I didn't like taught me skills that I could use later in jobs that I enjoyed more.

Your purpose or calling may involve doing unpaid volunteer work of some kind. Our purpose here, whether inside or outside an occupation, is to serve the greater good. It is this purpose, and not wealth, that you truly desire, and that you are truly seeking. How can you best connect with others to serve them? If you can make an income by doing work that allows you to express a greater purpose, you are very fortunate.

What do you desire to do, regardless of whether it provides income or not, that will benefit and positively affect others?

Persistence Is Required to Complete Your Goals

Was the information I learned in college useful and valuable? Some of it was. But more valuable was learning to complete goals—to finish projects, to research and write papers, to study for and pass tests. Learning those methods was more important than learning content.

Many of us can start projects, but finishing them is another story, not giving up when things get hard or challenging. At some point, almost any project will get challenging, especially near the very end. Crossing the finish line takes persistence, despite setbacks.

Try to solve every problem as it occurs, staying focused until your goal is achieved. The quality of persistence is found in all individuals who are successful, irrespective of their work. Finding others with skills we lack may be needed for us to complete a goal. When others' help is needed, persistence may be required to find that help. Persistence supersedes education and having connections. Having a mentor who coaches me and encourages me along the way to complete my goals has also helped me get to the finish line.

Chapter 15:
Clarity on Christianity

Accounts of Jesus in the Bible Were Not Written Down Until Decades After His Death

I didn't know that until I was in my late forties. When I found out, I asked a few other people if they knew about it, and it didn't seem to be common knowledge. The quotes and stories from accounts of Jesus were verbally passed on by word of mouth for forty to sixty-five years. Only then did those accounts get written down.

What happens to a story when it is passed from one person to another several times by word of mouth? The story changes a little each time it is told and retold. This is something that churches don't want to talk about, so you never hear much about it, since it brings the accuracy of the written content into question.

In reality, the word-of-mouth accounts were different forty to sixty-five years later when they were written down for the first time. But we just don't know how much they differed. It's not Jesus' fault that there were no video or voice recordings at the time. He just came to say, "Unconditionally give to and love each other, forgive each other unconditionally, and follow the Golden Rule." That's it. The original content and message were shaped and changed from word-of-mouth accounts over forty to sixty-five years, influenced by culture, politics, understanding, and interpretations of the times. So our job is to peel the onion to reach the core, to peel away all the layers of man's additional influences, which have caused misinterpretations of the simple core message. Some of man's influences on the message were caused by superstition, instinctual drives, political motivations, and limited knowledge of science and psychology. Religion itself is a man-made institution with selfish motives of power and money that corrupt the original message's interpretations and objectives.

The Core Message of Christianity

Beyond the misinterpretations and shortcomings of man, Christianity contains the core message of truth. The core of Jesus' message was based on unconditional giving, which includes forgiveness. He was saying, "What you give is what you get, so forgive each other." That is the core of what he was trying to tell us, and also show us through example. He was teaching us that simple principle through his stories, his parables, and his behavior. That's it. Give to one another unconditionally—meaning, love one another unconditionally.

Jesus lived above his own instinctual drives for sex and money. He was the ultimate example of a giver and forgiver. He gave unconditionally. Simply saying "I love you" is meaningless without actions to back it up. The action of love is in the giving to others, unconditionally. Jesus showed love through his actions. He gave to everyone unconditionally to show us that love is more than words—it needs to be performed. And he performed through his example at an ultimate level.

Human beings have used religion to justify war and killing in the name of Christianity. Would Jesus have endorsed that? Of course not. Is that God's will? No, it's man's will. Can we forgive the Church for its sins, arrogance, judgments, and ignorance? Can we forgive each other? We need to forgive in order to heal ourselves.

Christianity Has 30,000+ Versions, with Each Claiming Absolute Interpretation of the Truth

There are over 30,000 denominations or brands of Christianity, with each claiming to have a more accurate interpretation of it than the others. Each brand claims: "You have to interpret the Bible our way, or you are doing it wrong. You need to say the prayer exactly like this, or follow these exact rules, or you are not saved from hell in the afterlife." Are Catholics more right than Baptists? Each denomination will say it's so, and then argue if given the chance. Christianity has created more exclusion than inclusion within itself as a religion because human beings are tribal and like to pick sides and do the "I'm right and you're wrong" thing. Which branch is truly correct in interpretation, and why? Which are wrong, and why? Each Christian denomination claims to accurately interpret the truth. You know when you hear an interpretation that's not true. You may not know exactly how and why, but you know something is not right.

In the past, as I listened to someone evangelizing to me, I sometimes thought, *Something doesn't feel right here. I don't really believe what you just said. Some things you said don't make sense. Some parts yes, some parts no.*

But when I raised objections, I was told, "It's all true. You just need to accept it and believe it this way, because it's God's word. Your lack of understanding is the problem."

So, I am told to believe something without understanding it. Otherwise, I'm rejecting the word of God. Once I hear that, I want to reject the religion.

Why must the Bible be so complicated, such a puzzle with so many parables and contradictions? Because we like puzzles. Problems arise when people arrogantly claim to take every word in the Bible as literal truth.

There are some contradictions in the Bible when one compares the Old Testament with the New Testament—for example, "an eye for an eye," as opposed to "turn the other cheek." Which is correct, the old or the new? That is up to our interpretation and which parts of the Bible we choose to believe.

Many Christian denominations interpret the Bible using literal logic. But much of the Bible was written in the form of parables, which were simple stories used to illustrate a moral or spiritual lesson. Parables were the figurative way of telling a story during those times over two thousand years ago. They included the culture, beliefs, and superstitions of the times, and were written by imperfect men with motives based on selfish human instincts and politics. Instinctual drives and politics have continually influenced the interpretations of Christianity for over two thousand years.

It was only in 1692 and 1693 that the Salem witch trials took place in Massachusetts, and a Christian denomination accused over two hundred young women of practicing "the Devil's magic," after which it proceeded to hang nineteen of them and stone one to death. Did you believe they were burned? Until recently I did, too. Nope, they were hanged. And yet, many people have believed they were burned. Sometimes we believe things said by others that turn out not to be true. So, were those killings justified by true interpretations of the Bible? The people in that Christian denomination believed so.

It is up to you to filter out what is true from what is false—to decipher true meaning. Religions and churches have not yet delivered a perfect message.

Do you get the truth in church? Sure, you do. You get parts of it; you get pieces of it. But then you also get stuff that isn't the truth—man-made opinions with interpretations mixed in. Something always comes up to make you think, *Wait a second.... That's not true.* And then many people get confused, and ultimately reject religion, because they are asked to believe in an "all or nothing" sort of way—black-and-white, no grey. The majority of Christian denominations promote literal interpretations of the Bible as more correct and "right" than figurative interpretations.

Another point of confusion about Christianity is its hierarchy of good and evil entities. On the good side, there is the Holy Trinity: first, there's God the Father; then there's Jesus the Son of God; and then there's the Holy Spirit. In addition to those three, there are more deities to add to the list: angels, archangels, cherubim, and saints. Then, on the evil side, there are the Devil, evil spirits, and demons. At the end of our lives, our individual spirits are judged as good or evil, and are placed accordingly in heaven or hell. Before my own revelations, none of this rang completely true to me as it was explained, interpreted, and outlined. After my revelations, I clearly understood that there is a Great Spirit of One, the eternal—which in Christian terminology would be called the Holy Spirit.

The Bible is a complicated riddle that consists of many books that were written over a long period of time. Should it take a doctoral degree and special intelligence to figure it out and explain it to others? Some people say they have figured it out, but have they really? How do they express their interpretation of the Bible? Their living character is more powerful than their spoken interpretation. Actions speak louder than words; how do they treat others?

Religion's Rules, Traditions, and Rituals Were Not Part of Jesus' Message

I went to a nondenominational Christian church this morning, where the pastor was talking about how religion has created laws and rules, which is not what Jesus came here to teach us. Laws and rules open the doors to condemnation and judgment of others who aren't following those laws and rules—which create totally unnecessary barriers that do nothing to assist learning the truth of how to give unconditionally.

Christianity has split up into so many different versions, each with its own set of rules and traditions to follow, that people naturally take sides to argue. "I'm right, and you're wrong!" they say. That only promotes more tribal separation and division, not unity. Would Jesus be proud of the man-made religious institutions called Christianity today? We like to create divisions with each other because tribalism is an inseparable part of human nature.

Jesus himself was a Jew, who came to say that the old rules and traditions were not necessary. He never intended to start a new religion called "Christianity." He wanted to keep things simple. People decided otherwise, confusing his beautiful message, which is to give to others unconditionally and be of service to them, not ourselves. Jesus' message was about unity and acceptance, not division and judgment, which are a result of the rules and requirements of religions invented by man.

Catholicism created a "pope," a hierarchy of positions of power, and its own set of rules and traditions that are expected to be followed and obeyed by its followers. One of the rules calls for priests to remain celibate—but that attracted and protected pedophiles, who have abused their positions for centuries. Greed, lust, and abuse of power are challenges within all churches.

My First Attempt at "Getting Saved" Was in a Trailer Church in Louisiana

When I was seventeen years old, and living in Louisiana, I decided to get "saved." A friend had recommended a small church that held services in a trailer. So, one Sunday, I walked into the trailer church right in the middle of a service. I immediately saw two rows of folding chairs set up on the left and right, with a line of people standing down the middle. Everyone was waiting to go up to the front, where a preacher was laying his hands on the top of their heads and "speaking in tongues," a language I didn't understand. As the people in line got "saved," they would start shaking and fall to the ground, as if they were fainting and convulsing. They seemed to be taken over by some unseen power.

As I was waiting in line, I started to get nervous, for it appeared that I was finally going to know firsthand what getting saved was all about. I expected to become "filled with God" or to have the Holy Spirit "take me over." I was thinking, *I can't wait to feel this and to get God.*

When my turn finally came, I approached the preacher, who put his hands on my head and started to speak in tongues. But I didn't feel anything! I didn't feel the spirit entering my body. I didn't fall. I didn't shake. I kept expecting a feeling to come over me, but nothing happened.

I didn't move on, but just stood there, holding up the line. After the preacher removed his hands from my head, I waited for him to touch me on the head again. *Surely*, I thought, *he saw that nothing happened to me. Doesn't he realize that he needs to do it again?*

Finally, he had to gently push me out of the way, so he could move on to the next person. For a moment, I wanted to resist, and ask him to do it again, but I didn't. Returning to the back of the church, I sat down and continued to watch the other people having their "experience." I was about to go up again, but then I thought, *Am I the only one who's not getting it? Is it just me?*

The man in front of me in line had fallen down on the floor and fainted. The woman behind me in line had fallen to the floor and jerked around with her eyes closed. I thought, *Wait. I missed it.* Then I asked myself, *Do I get back in line and try again? I missed it. I didn't get it.* And my answer to myself was, *Something's going on here. Something's not right. Everybody's doing exactly the same thing. These people are faking it. They may have wanted the experience to be real so much that they were pretending to do what "getting the spirit" should look like. But it's not real.*

I was disappointed. From that experience forward in my life until my revelations, I lost any hope of truly connecting with God.

"Jesus, Save Me"—What Part Do I Play?

Most Christian denominations suggest, or even require, us to pray for "Jesus to save us." The belief is that, from that moment forward, you will be saved and forever forgiven. Does that mean that, no matter what choices you make in the future, you have just avoided eternal hell and damnation and been guaranteed a ticket to heaven? And you did that just by saying the prayer you were instructed to say? In other words, eternal salvation and avoidance of eternal damnation depend on one prayer? Is it really that black-and-white? Many people will tell you it is. But I could never believe that salvation is that simple. It didn't make sense, even if so many people believed it. But it does show how we all like short-cuts. People would rather take a diet pill than do the hard work of exercising.

But, yes, I can be "saved" by the truth, by shining a light on ignorance and lies—the lies of our selfish instinctual drives, which keep us blind to the truth and make us ignore our heart, which is God's guidance. That is what Jesus showed us how to do. He was a teacher who showed us by example what we can aspire to become. He showed us that it is possible to overcome our in-stinctual drives. Learning truth and wisdom from his example and teachings "saves us." But after hearing and learning these truths, it is up to us to apply them to our free-will choices in order for us to be "saved." That is how Jesus "saves." We choose our salvation, moment to moment. It is not a one-and-done deal.

A correct explanation of the "Jesus save me" prayer is that it is a verbal commitment to move forward with our own striving for the ideals taught by Jesus. The prayer is a promise to give unconditionally to others from the heart, as Jesus did. It is a vow to listen to the heart above the human flesh and the selfish desires of instinctual drives that cause us to harm others or ourselves. It means starting to make choices to give to others, to be of service to others, to deny and sacrifice our own needs and put the needs of others first. We make that commitment despite our instinctual drives, which tell us to be selfish, to only please ourselves, and to justify harming others in the process.

Making that commitment does not mean that now that we have said the "save me prayer," we no longer experience "hell" and pain when we make selfish choices that harm ourselves or others. There will still be a price to pay if we harm others. It is false to believe that, with one prayer, we can bypass all personal responsibility for our own salvation. Once we are exposed to the "truth," and we are no longer "ignorant," we have a personal responsibility to act accordingly. That requires effort and sacrifice on our part. There are no shortcuts to salvation. It is an ongoing effort.

We are "saved" when our choices reflect what Jesus taught about love and service. Being "saved" is ultimately up to our own free-will choices, which lead us to make unselfish decisions. Being kind, loving, patient, tolerant, and forgiving are all choices—just as being cruel, mean, intolerant, impatient, violent, and harmful are also free-will choices. Some choices result in hell on Earth, while other choices result in heaven on Earth.

It takes persistent effort to deny our own powerful instincts in order to not be selfish. Being "saved" does not remove our instinctual challenges. We have to continually choose to oppose our instinctual drives when they direct us to harm or neglect others. It's about us choosing with our own free will to give unconditionally, and to forgive, regardless of whether or not that is deserved. Jesus showed us in the past how to save ourselves, and by following his example, we can save ourselves in the present. It is up to us to follow his example in choosing unconditional giving and forgiving in order to save ourselves. That is how Jesus' example in the past saves us in the present.

People like to defend rigid interpretations of a simple message. Many people just go along with what they are told. They mimic believing what others believe, without understanding the meaning of it. Who wants to stand up and disagree with a whole group? And what happens when someone does that? It is easier to conform by just pretending to believe a certain way.

Jesus' example was to always give kindness and love to everyone, in all circumstances. He gave them the shirt off his back, or the shoes off his feet, whether or not they deserved it. He was the ultimate example of an Expert Giver. He showed us what is possible. But we have to do the footwork and make the choices to save ourselves from being in hell here in this life, and also to experience more of heaven here.

So, the instruction to be saved with a single prayer that tears up your ticket to hell and gives you a ticket to eternal paradise is false, because it assumes that you can go on sinning and harming others all you want with no consequence of hell. Whether you say that prayer or not, you will still experience hell on Earth in this life if you continue to harm and neglect others. The argument is that the prayer saves you from hell in an afterlife. But it's the hell in this life that we need to escape.

What Is Hell?

The mainstream Christian message is that if you don't get saved by saying one prayer at one point in time, you will go to hell after this life. Newsflash! Hell is an experience in this life, one we need to escape in the here and now in the human condition.

Hell is brought on in the present reality of our human lives by our instinctual drives that steer our choices into being selfish and hurting others or ourselves directly or indirectly. Pain and suffering are the result of those choices. Being afraid of "going" to hell later is missing the point. We need the truth that will help us to overcome the hell we experience in the here and now in this life.

The main scriptural misinterpretation of hell is that punishment comes in an afterlife, not in this life. But hell is about *this* life. The consequences of living in hell in our human life result from harming or neglecting others in the here and now. Our challenge is to escape the hell we experience in this life, and move into creating more heaven on Earth, by giving to others unconditionally and serving them.

Our motives for being unselfish should not be driven by fear of punishment after this life. Hell does not come in the afterlife. Hell comes in this life. When we die as human beings, we don't take our bodies with us. Our human ego, with its wants, drives, and selfishness, dies. Many people cannot let go of the human form when they imagine life after death. But our essence, which is One with the Great Spirit, lives on into eternity without our human forms.

If we are stuck in selfishness, serving only our selfish instinctual drives while disregarding and harming ourselves and others in the process, we are damned to hell in the here and now. Our primary goal is to choose with our free will to shape this reality we are in with our human life, to bring it closer to heaven—to evolve.

What Is Sin?

The Seven Deadly Sins include lust, gluttony, greed, sloth, wrath, envy, and pride. I will add a few more: jealousy, doubt, worrying, and controlling. To sin is to operate from our instinctual drives, our preprogrammed human natures, to the detriment of others and ourselves, creating hell on Earth. Do we all sin? Of course, we do. We all have instinctual drives. We always will.

One example of sin is lust. But lust in itself is not sinful. Lust is a natural desire, with its primary purpose being procreation, and its secondary purpose being intimate connection with another person, which can be extremely enjoyable. In these instances, lust is not a sin. However, if lust drives us into selfishly harming others or ourselves, it is a sin. Primary examples of lust becoming sin include rape and pedophilia.

Christianity's Mainstream Interpretation of "Jesus Died for Our Sins"

Jesus died the way he did to give us an important message—one we need the most. He showed us how to forgive the ignorant. He died painfully, and wrongfully, but still he was kind, loving, tolerant, and forgiving. He died in order to show us what is possible as human beings. He did not judge us, when he would have been completely justified in doing so, because he wanted to relay a powerful message to all of us forever. He was hoping that by witnessing his words of forgiveness while he was suffering on the cross, we would learn how to give and forgive unconditionally.

By sacrificing his life, Jesus showed us that forgiveness is possible in any circumstance. That was the whole point of his message, which he gave by his example on the way out. He died in forgiveness of us—the "us" who crucified the ultimate Expert Giver. Jesus showed us how to solve the puzzle here. He was the one human being who was guilty of no sin, no harm to others in any way. Yet, we crucified him, and when we did that, he forgave us.

What does "Jesus died for our sins" mean? Those words have always confused me. Jesus' actions were a true reflection of his words. He lived without the sins of lust, gluttony, greed, sloth, wrath, envy, or pride. He did no harm to anyone. He lived above his instinctual drives for sex and money, above hate and revenge, and above the shortcomings of natural human characteristics, to teach us by his example and testimony how to give unconditionally, and how to forgive unconditionally, which is the most important lesson we are here to learn.

The phrase *Jesus died for our sins* is misunderstood by many people. It does not mean that, because he died, I can sin all I want without consequence—as if Jesus' dying for my sins gives me a free pass to sin all I like, and I'm forgiven with no hell to pay. That doesn't make sense. Some people like that interpretation, because it takes personal responsibility and accountability off their shoulders. But that interpretation is neither correct nor useful. Our continuous choices followed by action are required for our salvation in the here and now from our selfish instinctual drives.

Salvation is maintained, not won with a prayer. It is not a get-out-of-jail-free card with no action required. Faith without works is dead. The misinterpretation is that we don't have to do the "work," because Jesus did it all for us—as if we can do whatever we want and get away with it, because Jesus paid the price for us, and now we can sin and harm others all we want. There are no shortcuts to salvation without real effort on our part. There is no getting something for nothing. Change in our behavior is essential.

Jesus showed us what to do and how to do it. That does not mean that he will continue to do it for us in the present. Remember, Jesus said, "Be healed and go and sin no more." What does that mean? It means that, from this moment on, you go forward knowing the truth and give unconditionally to others. You do not live a self-centered life, harming or neglecting others, allowing your instinctual drives, the Devil, to dominate you. It means that every intention you have, and every action you take that involves other people, needs to benefit others in some way, and not just yourself. Because the true reality is that when you give to others, you are giving to yourself because we are all part of One. That is why the Golden Rule is true. Jesus knew this and showed us that he knew it through his example.

Actions speak louder than words. Jesus had every right to be angry at the people who condemned him at the end. He could have said, "I give up on all of you. You are hopeless." But he didn't do that, because that would have corrupted his message. Instead, he did the most unimaginable thing from a human perspective, something that goes against all logic to anyone who witnessed it or learned about it later. He forgave us.

Jesus was innocent of any crimes. He was the perfect example of our potential. Despite that, he was beaten, bludgeoned, and crucified until he died. In the midst of his pain and suffering, before dying on the cross, Jesus said, "Father, forgive them, for they know not what they do." He died without complaining, or being angry, or condemning anyone. He showed us, in an extreme way, how to forgive. In dying, he showed us that forgiveness is always possible, under any circumstances.

That is how Jesus "died for our sins." Our sins were to kill an innocent person, who sacrificed himself and died to teach us how to give and forgive. Up to the very end, he taught us that by his example. So Jesus died "forgiving us of our sin of killing him." That is the notion of forgiveness of sins. Jesus forgave. He was above sin. He showed us how to forgive, even when that is undeserved.

Because of his act, the responsibility falls on us to follow his example of forgiveness and to love others.

Jesus never gave in. He never said, "I condemn you. I judge you." Right up until his death, he was an example of tolerance and forgiveness. Jesus chose to die the way he did, to relay a lasting message to mankind. He didn't get angry. He just said, in effect, "I know you don't really understand what you're doing, but I love you anyway, and I forgive you." That's how he died—by being an example of how to operate above our sins and our human traits, which direct us to hurt each other and hold resentments. Jesus knew the truth that man did not know: We are all One, but just ignorant of this in our human condition.

Grace, Karma, and Forgiveness of Sins

Karma defined:

- *(In Hinduism and Buddhism:) the sum of a person's actions in this and previous states of existence, viewed as deciding their fate in future existences.*

In other words, what you give now is what you get back—later. Christianity's message that "We reap what we sow" and the "karma" of Hinduism and Buddhism are closely related. They both contain the notion that our future depends on what we do in the present.

Grace defined:

- *(In Christian belief:) the free and unmerited favor of God, as manifested in the salvation of sinners and the bestowal of blessings.*

Grace is undeserved forgiveness. Once we begin choosing to unconditionally give to others and to forgive them, "grace" comes in to pay our debts for past pain we have caused others. In Christianity, grace is "forgiveness of our sins." It is connected to our unselfishly choosing to serve others. And by our going in this new direction, grace forgives some or all of what we deserve back from our past sins. We are forgiven when we forgive others. Grace is a gift that forgives past sins in exchange for current ongoing giving to others and forgiving of others, which encourages our path toward evolution and awakening.

Two Thousand Years Ago, Selfish Instinctual Drives Were Defined as the Devil

How did people think about human drives and instincts that led us to harm and neglect others two thousand years ago? Myth and superstition were common in those times.

Literal language uses words and phrases to mean exactly what they say. Figurative language uses words and phrases in analogous senses, not exact ones. Analogous means comparable in certain respects, typically in ways that clarify the nature of things being compared. Some figurative descriptions of the Devil might include:

The Devil is the lie that we are just our individual ego, separate from everyone and everything else.

The Devil is ego ignoring the Great Spirit or the heart's desires.

The Devil is denial that we are One, and that whatever I do to you, I am really doing to myself.

The Devil is self-centeredness, greed, jealousy, envy, revenge, gluttony, harmful lust, and arrogance.
The Devil is choosing to harm others and ourselves.
The Devil is every human being on the planet to varying
degrees.

The words that Jesus used to describe our instinctual drives
that create our harmful selfish natures and choices were *Satan* and
the *Devil*. Jesus used that terminology in a figurative manner to
describe and define instinctual drives to people of his time, to explain how those drives influence us to cause harm to others and to
make selfish, unforgiving choices. Back then, people didn't have
the full understanding or the correct terminology to explain their
selfish instinctual drives, so they used figurative explanations.
Jesus was attempting to define the problem and the cause of the
problem in a way that made sense to the people of that time.

But many Christians today still interpret descriptions of the
Devil and Satan in a completely literal way, which promotes the
concept of blaming our harmful selfish actions and choices on
something else outside ourselves, shifting personal responsibility
away from ourselves onto a deity, the Devil. This literal interpretation of the Devil not only encourages the idea that we are victims of forces outside ourselves, but also creates in us a sense of
powerlessness and unnecessary fear.

Two thousand years ago, the concept of the Devil, or Satan,
was an attempt to explain evil, selfish, harmful free will choices
made by man, which originate from the instinctual challenges of
the human experience. Fortunately, in the bigger picture, we are
not slaves to an evil force behind the scenes. However, we often
do become slaves to an evil force in this realm, and it's the force

of our own natures, which was put there by design to ensure our survival on Earth as humans.

But the natural forces that direct our survival as humans can demand more than is necessary, and can lead to justifying selfish trends in behavior at the peril of others. We commit evil when our instinctual drives and ambitions take over and rule us and our actions, causing us to disregard the welfare of others. The battle against evil is actually a battle within ourselves and against our own human instinctual drives. The solution to this battle is to learn how and why our instinctual drives control us, and then to choose to oppose them. This is commonly called the battle between flesh and spirit.

Two thousand years ago, these cunning, powerful, persuasive forces were explained as being caused by the deity "Satan." Our challenge is to understand that we are much more than our shouting, demanding, screaming, dominant instinctual drives. To evolve here, we need to listen to the soft whisper of our heart, the one that says to serve others, give to others, sacrifice for others, and have empathy and compassion for others. That involves ignoring the unrelenting selfish instinctual drives and demands for excess and *not* making choices that harm ourselves and others— which is to deny Satan. Our instincts, which strive to exceed their proper function, can cause us to justify cruel, mean, and selfish behaviors. This is our primary challenge to overcome.

Evil is a human experience. Its roots lie in our selfishness as a primary directive for survival. This directive is driven by hormones and instinctual programming to sustain life in the form we experience it. Selfishness ensures that we stay alive longer. All humans have the option to express evil. Our own inclinations to choose evil, and to deal with others who choose evil, are part of the challenge we have as humans. Those inclinations are part of the ride we are on in this life. Evil is a human challenge, and something we are all capable of choosing. Our built-in guidance system of love, which is to sacrifice and be of service to others, is weak compared to our instincts and hormonal drives, which direct us to be "evil," or to harm and neglect others. Satan, our selfish instinctual drives, is not easy to overcome. Our challenge to evolve requires us to choose to be less and less selfish—to choose not to harm each other, regardless of feeling like doing so; to forgive when it is not what we want to do.

Some point their finger and say, "The Devil made me do it. It would be so much easier to be giving if the Devil weren't influencing me to be selfish. The Devil and the evil spirits are responsible when I'm selfish and choose to harm others. They are to blame for my evil acts!"

Those are some of the lies we tell ourselves so we can play the victim—just some of the excuses we use to justify selfish or harmful behavior concerning others. However, those excuses are based on ignorance and misinterpretation. Ignorance can be overcome with truth. So consider that possibility: that for the first time you will know the truth that there is no Devil deity to blame. People make evil choices with their own free will.

Some of our evil choices may be caused by:

- The influence of drugs such as cocaine, methamphetamine, narcotics, and alcohol.
- Hormonal imbalances.
- Brain structure abnormalities.
- Chronic stress that causes frontal lobe neuronal shrinkage from frequent exposure to the stress hormone cortisone,

which leads to lowered compassion and empathy.
- Past abuse or lack of love in our lives.
- Redirecting onto others the pain we have experienced in the past.

When I see people with a negative personality interacting with others, I wonder who it was in their past who treated them that way. Who are they mimicking? It is usually a parent who had that influence. In any case, the blame lands on ourselves as individuals, and we will pay the consequences directly or indirectly for the choices we make. People harming others directly or indirectly will experience pain themselves as a result. We want to blame others, or deities, for our problems and our selfish behavior because it's not natural to look for fault in ourselves.

We want someone or something else to blame for our selfish behavior. It's ugly, so we need to blame it on others or a Devil because we don't want to blame ourselves. We need to be the victim, so we can shift responsibility away from ourselves. Having a deity on which to blame our choices that harm or neglect others does provide a convenient scapegoat, so we can avoid personal responsibility.

"The Devil made me do it."

"It's not my fault…, it's their fault…, or your fault."

"Something or someone else made me do it."

"I'm a victim."

Blaming others is the standard in today's world. But you won't experience true happiness in this life so long as you are blaming the Devil or others for your selfish choices. Taking responsibility and personal accountability requires humility, which is one of mankind's greatest challenges.

As humans, however, we need our instinctual drives to function and survive. Human existence requires some degree of selfishness to survive, procreate, find food, make shelter, keep going, and stay alive. But instincts can become the Devil when they completely drive our motives, causing us to justify hurting others to get what we want. I am the Devil when I'm blindly led to excess pursuits by my instincts, which compel me to justify harming others or ignoring their needs. One example of our selfishness and neglect of each other is the lack of clean drinking water for over six hundred million people on Earth. We have the resources to correct that problem, but we don't. We actively turn away and ignore suffering. We usually don't act or deal with it unless we have to, or it affects us directly.

Our instinctual drives can seem like a force in themselves, separate from "us." For the most part, they do drive us from a subconscious level. But those drives are coming from the human part of us, not the spiritual part. Yes, we can be "possessed" by our instincts blindly ruling us, causing us to make cruel and greedy choices—that is, to act like the Devil.

But we are not "victims" of a "Devil." We have the responsibility in our choices to follow instinctual drives to excess or not. It is our choice, and the blame is on ourselves. Our consequences are the price we pay for our choices, which are the hell or heaven we experience in this life.

When people act like the Devil, they are not listening to their heart deep down within them. They are ignoring their heart, and by doing that they lack empathy for others and fail to provide any service to others that doesn't involve some selfish gain or return for themselves. Being the Devil is painful, for it creates hell on Earth.

In the Year 2000, I Learned the Truth About the "Devil"

We like to worship our own egos and praise ourselves. Some of us like to show off to others how much we have in the way of material possessions. But showing off creates envy and jealousy in others, which only separates us further and further from each other. To advertise and promote an elevated status does not create deeper or more meaningful connections with others.

I reached the pinnacle of that ignorant point in my own life more than eighteen years ago. From being a giver throughout my twenties, helping other people and being of service to others, I became selfish when I hit thirty. What happened? I chose to start an internet-based company of women on webcams around the world. At the time, I justified to myself that it wasn't a bad thing to do. Of course, that was before I had a daughter of my own. My justification to myself at the time was that the girls were over 18, and the work was very lucrative for them, too. I knew it wasn't the right thing to do for various reasons, but I was in a rebellious mode and chose to do it anyway.

During my time in that company, I became selfish and self-centered. It was as if I had forgotten how to give. The knowledge of how to give to others was just a dream from the past. I had become solely focused on myself, on making money, and on self-gratification. I became an expert taker, focused on gratifying myself. I focused on dating, buying more things for myself, and personal hobbies for distracting and entertaining myself. For two years, I lived on a yacht, and was dating multiple women. But was I happy? No. I was more chronically dissatisfied than I had ever been up to that point in my life. Why? Because everything was about me. I wasn't giving. I was selfish and living for my own gratification. I just focused on myself without thinking about others or serving others. My life became empty, depressing, and unsatisfying. My life was about getting what I wanted to get, rather than about what I wanted to give. As I became less and less giving, the feelings of peace, serenity, and joy completely eluded me.

I found that having more money and more stuff only meant that I had more to worry about losing, and more to protect. I also experienced more envy and jealousy from others, which meant more isolation and separation. Insanity. Confusion. Lying to myself. I was blindly going deeper in a direction that only became more and more painful.

Two and a half years after starting that company, I was at a strip club one night. I remember that I was so miserable and unsatisfied with life, although I theoretically "had it all." It was in that strip club that I stood up, raised my hands above my head, and shouted out, like a prayer: "If there's a Satan, come to me and help me grow my power in this world! Come to me now and give me more power!"

I said that in rebellion against God, for I was mad at God. How absurd. God didn't do this to me. God didn't leave me. I had left God.

Guess what happened right after I said that prayer?

A soft, calm, clear, peaceful, and very loving voice spoke to me out loud inside my head. It said, "You're doing this to yourself. It's you."

Wow! God had spoken to me! There was no Satan or feeling of Satan that came to me. Satan did not exist outside of me. Satan was not there. He didn't exist, or I certainly would have felt his presence. I had been completely sincere in my request to

Satan. And God spoke to me after that moment, and the message was crystal clear. I realized right after that moment that I had already become Satan myself, a fallen angel. I had chosen separation from God, my heart; my selfish instinctual drives were ruling me.

Where I was in my life, and how I felt about life and myself at the time, were all caused by living 100 percent selfishly for my instinctual gratification. There was no Devil or Satan to blame it on. It was my own free will and ignorance that were totally running the show. I was seeking my own pleasure, and I had lost the ability to give. I was blinded by selfishness. I had been ignoring my heart for some time. The more I got, the more I wanted to try to fill the hole—but the hole just got wider and deeper.

It is impossible to fill a spiritual hole with people and things. When your life is all about pursuing fulfillment of selfish instinctual demands of getting, you need more, more, more. The world says that that is the answer. Our instincts say that that's the answer. But that's not true. It's a lie. The truth is the opposite. I needed to give, but I had forgotten how. I was trapped in selfishness, in lying to myself, in my ignorance, dominated by my instincts. My selfish instinctual demands were screaming all the time, clouding out the faint whimpers of my heart. By the way, that's hell. I was in hell right here on Earth.

So, eighteen years ago, I learned that there is no Devil—that *I* had become the Devil. I was the fallen angel, separated from God by denying my heart. The voice of God, the Spirit of One, which came through my heart, was a loving, calm, patient, and kind voice, which told me the truth that night. That was my first profound spiritual experience and lesson.

"Jesus Is the Only Way"

Recently, while I was driving, I passed a church sign that said, "Joy is only found through Jesus." I know what they really meant to say is, "Joy is only found through what Jesus taught us about unconditional giving and forgiveness, through his parables and his examples, and through the teaching and examples of his core message, before it was corrupted and misinterpreted by human beings and religion." The message Jesus taught and demonstrated, his core message of the Golden Rule, is also expressed in other religions besides Christianity. To treat others as I wish to be treated means to unconditionally give to and forgive others. Coming to know the core truth of the Golden Rule gives us the reason to listen to our heart and ignore our powerful selfish instinctual drives.

But Jesus said, "I am the way, and the truth, and the life. No one comes to the Father except through me." He was saying that there is only one truth. And that one truth and one way is to unconditionally give to others, and unconditionally forgive others. That unconditional giving and forgiving is the only way and truth. There is no other way. Jesus was not defending all of the future Christian denominations, which he did not recommend or promote, but were created and defended by human beings. The core truth that Jesus shared does exist in other religions and in other sources of information.

When Christians proclaim that "Jesus is the only way," that is taking an "It's my way or the highway" stance, which only serves to create a barrier to entry with an argument that is based on a limited inaccurate interpretation. Most people who want to argue claim that the truth is not found anywhere else except in Christianity. But the truth is the truth, even when it is available through other sources. A misdirected argument is to say that if you get the truth from another source, you will not be saved. Instead, you will be condemned to hell in an afterlife unless you understand the truth through a Christian interpretation. Furthermore, those rules apply differently throughout the different denominations of Christianity. When outsiders observe this behavior, most of them see it as ridiculous, judgmental, and arrogant.

If you learn about the Golden Rule from a source outside of Christianity, and then you live your life abiding by that Rule, will you be damned to hell? I think if Jesus saw people following those truths now, such as Buddhist monks, he would not have any problem or dispute with them. Remember, Jesus did not start a religion called Christianity. That was man's idea. Jesus said, "I am the way." He was not saying that if you find "the way" through another source, that's not right. That would be arguing just for the sake of arguing. Of course, people *do* love to argue.

Jesus was the ultimate example and teacher of the Golden Rule. He showed everyone that the truth and the way that we need to learn to solve the puzzle here is to rise above our instincts (our sins or selfish drives that cause harm to others), and follow our heart's guidance, which is to serve others, and not just ourselves. Jesus promoted compassion, understanding, humility, patience, kindness, sacrifice, and forgiveness. Unconditional giving, love, and forgiveness *are* the only way to attain spiritual awakening. But this perfect truth that Jesus taught is not perfectly represented by any Christian denomination created by human beings.

In Matthew 7:12 (NIV), the Golden Rule is expressed as follows: "So in everything, do to others what you would have them do to you, for this sums up the law and the prophets." Here are how some other religions express the same teaching:

143

Baha'i: Lay not on any soul a load that you would not wish to be laid upon you, and desire not for anyone the things you would not desire for yourself.

— Baha'u'llah Gleanings

Buddhism: Treat not others in ways that yourself would find hurtful. Do not offend others, as you would not like to be offended.

—Udana-Varga 5.18

Confucianism: One phrase which sums up the basis for all good conduct... loving kindness. Do not do to others what you would not want done to yourself.

—Confucius, Analects 15:23

Hinduism: This is the sum of duty: do not do to others what would cause pain if done to you.

—Mahabharata 5:15

Islam: Not one of you truly believes until you wish for others what you wish for yourself.

—The Prophet Mohammed, Hadith

Jainism: One should treat all creatures in the world as one would like to be treated.

—Mahavira, Sutravitanga

Judaism: What is hateful to you, do not do to your neighbor. This is the whole Torah; all the rest is commentary. What you do not wish for yourself, do not wish for others.

—Hillel, Talmad, Shabbat 31a

Maya: You are myself. We are all one.

—Popol Vuh

Native Spirituality: We are as much alive as we keep the earth alive.

—Chief Dan George

Sikhism: I am a stranger to no one; and no one is a stranger to me. Indeed, I am a friend to all.

—Guru Granth Sahib, p. 1299

Taoism: Regard your neighbor's gain as your own gain, and your neighbor's loss as your own loss.

—T'ai Shang Kan Ying P'ien, 213–218

Unitarianism: We affirm and promote respect for the interdependence of all existence of which we are a part.

—Unitarian principle

Zoroastrianism: Do not unto others what is injurious to yourself.

—Shayast-na-Shayast 13.29

The Prayer of St. Francis, below, sums up the entire core message of the Golden Rule:

Lord, make me an instrument of Thy peace;
where there is hatred, I may bring love;
where there is injury, I may bring pardon;
where there is doubt, I may bring faith;
where there is despair, I may bring hope;
where there is darkness, I may bring light;
and where there is sadness, I may bring joy.
O Divine Master,
grant that I may not so much seek to be consoled, as to console;
to be understood, as to understand;
to be loved, as to love;
for it is in giving that we receive,
it is in pardoning that we are pardoned,
it is in dying that we are born to eternal life.

In the last line of this prayer, Francis is referring to a transition and awakening in our current life.

Become Like Children Again—Return to Innocence

Jesus said in Matthew 18:3 (NIV), "I tell you the truth, unless you change and become like little children, you will never enter the kingdom of heaven." What did he mean?

As children, we are innocent. Then, when we become adults, we lose our innocence. What does losing our innocence mean? Many of us, as we enter adulthood, lose trust from being hurt by others, and become more guarded and fearful. Loss of innocence is also caused by hormonal changes that occur when we begin puberty, which activates sexual instincts and drives that weren't there before. Then, as we move past puberty into adulthood, financial security comes into play as we have to provide for ourselves. Usually, we need to start earning money in some way to meet our basic needs, and possibly the needs of others. Instinctual drives after puberty, the drives for sex and financial security, are the two forces that primarily take our innocence away. As we transition from childhood innocence to adulthood, our giving transforms from unconditional to conditional, based on having new instinctual drive motives concerning sex and financial security.

But how do we get back to being innocent? Can we become like children again? Can we take the risk of trusting again?

After puberty, we cannot return to the innocence of childhood without the challenges of instinctual drives. But we can become aware of those challenges, and not allow them to influence our choices. We can choose to oppose selfish or harmful urges, and to trust others despite our fears.

Animals lose their innocence, too, as they grow into adults. You can see that, for example, with lion cubs. You can interact with cubs, since they are playful, trusting, and loving. But as they reach maturity, with hormonal changes, their instinctual drives to hunt and kill develop, which may direct them to maul or kill you. Sometimes lions remember humans who handled them as cubs, and still welcome them with love, instead of instinctually attacking, even after they have been put back in the wild for years.

There is a beautiful love story about this kind of human-animal relationship that did continue over time. Search for "Christian the Lion" on YouTube to watch the video. When Christian meets his handler from years before, he maintains his cub innocence to operate from his heart, rather than from his instinctual drives. This reunion shows that even a lion can choose to return to innocence and love far into adulthood, despite its wild predator nature. If a lion can sometimes do this despite its instincts, so can we. Returning to innocence is listening to the heart, trusting the heart over our instincts and fears.

The Core Message Is That "Simple" Works: Focus on One Thing and Do It Well

Just look at Google. Google is simple. In the beginning, we had many choices of search engines. When the internet first arrived, search engines were a new field, with Google and Yahoo as the big two. They were both big at first, right? But Google was very simple, with the only option on the homepage being search. Yahoo, on the other hand, tried to be everything on its homepage: search, news, weather, entertainment, stocks, sports, etc. But as I went to Yahoo to search, I was confronted with information overload, and I had trouble just finding the search bar. As a result, over time, I only went to Google to search. It was easy. Google figured out that simple works.

Even as Google added news, weather, etc., later, they smartly kept it hidden and secondary to its primary function of search. A principle that I learned in business school was to do one thing and do it really well. Don't spread yourself too thin. Focus on what you're good at and what is your niche service. If you're in the restaurant business, stick with the food industry, which is the field you know best. Don't try to open a golf course if don't know golf. Stick with what you know best, so you can be really good in your area of expertise, instead of being somewhat good at many things. It's called niche focus. So, what does all this have to do with Christianity?

The Christian religions have not kept the core message of unconditional giving, love, and forgiveness a simple one. Would Jesus approve of what's become of his message? Human beings, via creating the religion called Christianity, with all its various denominations, have complicated and confused the simple concept and message of how to give and forgive unconditionally. Jesus did not intend to have all the confusion, rules, traditions, judgments, restrictions, or barriers to understanding the truth. Religion has confused what he meant to be a very simple message, which would require great humility from religious leaders to admit. Those who do will be my greatest heroes.

Oxymoron: A Wealthy Spiritual Leader

Some leaders in the church justify accumulating wealth from others' tithings. Was Jesus wealthy? Did he seek wealth and justify it, or promote a lifestyle of wealth and excess? Any excessively wealthy Christian leader is not a true example or interpreter of the real message that Jesus came to deliver.

When an individual takes a vow of poverty, he or she chooses to renounce personal worldly possessions and rely on communal sharing of resources. I don't expect all Christian leaders to take a vow of poverty, or to live lives of suffering and go without by living in poverty. At the same time, they absolutely should not obtain excessive personal wealth by collecting and using tithings, justifying this behavior by asserting that God wants them to "live abundantly." That is disgraceful in a world where so many people are suffering and being neglected while their basic needs are unmet. I do believe it would make Jesus angry and sad to witness this kind of hypocrisy. Excessive wealth-building and lavish lifestyles by church leaders who collect tithings are not something that Jesus would approve of. They are not examples of the Christianity we need in this world.

All this is not to say that accumulating wealth is bad if it is acquired in business, only that it is unacceptable if it is acquired through religious contributions and tithings, because it breaks a trust with the givers, since the money is not spent for its announced purposes.

Despite Its Shortcomings, Christianity Gives Big

Who does the most giving on a voluntary basis, aside from the government programs for the needy? Christians do. Christian churches give more, overall, than any other institution on a voluntary basis to help those in need throughout the world.

Actions Speak Louder Than Words

So far in my life, the best examples I have encountered of Christian faith have been those people who helped me and loved me with their actions—the ones who showed up during my struggles and gave to me with their time and resources. Their actions and their living examples spoke louder to me than their words. They are not talkers—they are doers. Anyone can say words. But what are their motives? Are they unselfish or selfish? Truly effective examples of Christianity do not have to say a word about the Bible or their religion. What you do matters more than what you say. The most powerful teachers in my life have been those who demonstrated their faith to me through example. I watched them give unconditionally, forgive unconditionally, and consistently be kind and patient to me and others. I especially admire those who are humble, giving and forgiving when no one is watching.

What Is God's Will?

Our human instinctual drives direct us to satisfy "our will," to take and not give, to be selfish.

Religions claim to know and profess "God's will," but they do this primarily through literal interpretations of texts that were written in the distant past.

Simply put, "God's will" is our heart's will. It requests sacrifice from us to be of service to others and to forgive others. It wants us to overcome our selfish directives, which means not allowing our selfish instinctual desires for sex and financial security to dominate and control our choices, decisions, and actions. Jesus was an example of someone doing God's will in human history.

In Matthew 6:9-12 (NIV), the Lord's Prayer reads: "Our Father in heaven, hallowed be your name, your kingdom come, your will be done, on earth as it is in heaven. Give us today our daily bread. And forgive us our debts, as we also have forgiven our debtors."

How many of us have forgiven our debtors? Most of us don't. That is real-deal unconditional giving. Matthew 6:13 (NIV) continues: "And lead us not into temptation, but deliver us from the evil one"—which happens to be our own selfish human instinctual desires, which justify us to harm others, ignoring our heart. We either make choices with our free will directed by our selfish human instinctual desires, or we make unselfish choices guided by our heart, which is God's will.

God's will is for us to unconditionally give in service to others, with no motive for sex or money in return. It is a choice that involves the sacrifice of self.

Prayer

***Prayer* defined:**
- *A solemn request for help or expression of thanks addressed to God or an object of worship.*
- *An earnest hope or wish.*

Prayer has three purposes:
1. To ask for help and intuitive guidance that is beyond human understanding, which requires faith and humility.
2. To express gratitude to something greater than one's ego.
3. To state an intention or goal for creation.

Letting go of your past prejudice toward religion and toward people who claim to represent God is the greatest challenge to becoming open to giving prayer a chance. If you never make the choice to try prayer, how can you determine its validity? Without trying, you are dismissing the practice of prayer based only on your judgment, not on your personal experience. Praying builds your faith. No one can give you faith. You will never know if a prayer is answered if you never pray in the first place. Noticing an answer will build your faith—the faith that you are actually getting help from something greater than yourself that you will never fully understand.

In general, prayer requests God to do something beyond your power to perform, either for others or for yourself. It is a humble submission and request to something greater than and beyond your ego identity, which is the Spirit of One. The very act of praying is humble in nature, regardless of your specific beliefs about God. The act of prayer is a humble admission that your ego is not

God, in and of itself. Praying is requesting help outside of "yourself," which is beyond your "ego identity."

If you pray, do you pray for yourself or for others? Are your prayers selfish "getting" requests to help yourself, or unselfish "giving" requests to help others? Any time you pray for someone else, or for them to heal or rise out of pain in some way, that is powerful. You are "heard." Your intent and will are heard. And behind the scenes, the wheels start turning. Thoughts and words have power. Let's say, for example, that you pray to help people to improve in some way. Perhaps you want to help them heal. Your prayer and intent are powerful when your will is in line with God's will. When you intend to benefit the greater whole, you sometimes get help from beyond your "self," when your good intentions line up with the *actual* benefit for the greater good. Meaning, sometimes our intentions may seem "good" on the surface, but we may not understand that our wishes are not aligned with the larger orchestration of God's will, a plan that benefits the greater good.

Do you pray to help others? Or do you pray only to get out of a jam, or for things you want? How many of us pray for others? How many of us only pray for ourselves, or for some selfish desire that has nothing to do with helping anyone else? Thinking of others is mostly secondary to all of us. But is that working in this world? What it comes down to is that prayer sets intentions. When I pray, I am asking a mysterious power greater than my "self" to help create an outcome. But my prayer has power only when it lines up with the will of the Spirit of One.

I can also "pray" for negative things to happen, such as for someone to get hurt. But that is not God's will or my heart's will. That is my human selfish instinctual will. That is an evil prayer. I won't get help from an evil prayer, because that is purely my

153

selfish will, which doesn't benefit the whole, or everyone. Prayer is only effective when I align God's will, my heart's will, with my will.

When we pray for harm to another, we only bring harm to ourselves, not the other person. Behind the scenes, the overall goal is that everyone should benefit. That's why selfish prayers are not empowered by God the way unselfish prayers are when they align with the greater spiritual will and plan.

I am a being here on Earth, with free will and free choice. As such, I can choose to ask the mysterious God for advice, wisdom, direction, and support beyond my own capabilities. I can choose to do that without a clear definition of God, and without any religious instruction whatsoever. I can choose to practice, seek, and have faith in the mysterious.

Remember, prayer is not about getting selfish desires met. Prayer is effective for meeting your basic needs and for increasing your ability to be of service to others. God is not Santa Claus.

I do ask the mysterious force beyond my human self for strength, guidance, and wisdom. Thanks to my revelations, I know that that mysterious Great Spirit of One is there with subtle guidance and support. Unless you have a direct experience of the supernatural, and you know of its existence with certainty, you will need faith and humility to begin praying. Prayer is a conscious acknowledgment of faith. With humility and open-mindedness, prayer can become an option for a trial run.

When I pray, I don't follow any religious rules. Sometimes I choose to ask for help, direction, and aid that I don't have myself. But even without prayer, my heart is always trying to instruct me on how to evolve in a way that benefits the greater good.

A Method of Meditation I Find Easy to Do

Why meditate? Ultimately, if it is successfully practiced, meditation provides an escape from your self, ego, individual identity, and the illusion of separation. It can be used to back out of this false reality of self and separation, to experience the spiritual connectedness to everything. It can allow you to experience your "oneness" of being. Experiencing that state provides temporary relief from your fears, stresses, and selfish ego desires. Here is one example of meditation that is cited in the Bible: "Be still and know that I am God" (Psalms 46:10, NIV).

For most of my life, I believed that meditation was an attempt to clear my mind of thoughts and keep it clear by using deep-breathing practices. I tried focusing on deep breaths in and out, but that method wasn't clearing my thoughts, so in frustration I gave up on practicing. Then I came across another technique that worked better for clearing my thoughts for longer periods—enough to reach the goal, however brief, of obtaining perfect peace. The practice involves choosing a two-syllable sound that has no meaning. Some examples could be: "taa-kah" or "sha-rah." Just find a two-syllable sound that you like, which has no meaning to you at all. Play around for one minute with meaningless two-syllable sounds that come to mind, and choose one. Now repeat "your" sound slowly, over and over, first out loud, and then silently.

Repeating a two-syllable sound with no meaning allows the brain to focus on one thing, which distracts it from thinking about anything else. I have also used the sound "ommm" successfully. With practice, an autopilot inside you will take over repeating the sound. That can be done in any environment and any position.

Initially, thoughts may interrupt your practice, but don't judge

155

them. Let them come and go. If one occurs, go back to focusing on the two-syllable sound with no meaning, over and over again, calmly, in repetition. Over time, fewer thoughts will interrupt your two-syllable sound repetition. By doing this practice, your brain will experience a deep level of rest. You will back away on autopilot, and experience peace that exists beyond your self and ego, and you may also glimpse your connection to everything as One.

I usually practice this meditation for fifteen to twenty minutes at a time. You can do it anywhere, even in distracting noisy environments. Just close your eyes and begin.

The Goal Is Progress, Not Perfection

Perfection is defined as "the condition, state, or quality of being free or as free as possible from all flaws or defects." The perfect goal in life would be to strive to always treat others as you want to be treated by them, regardless of your moods or your instinctual selfish drives, continually operating with the greater good in mind. However, perfection is never fully achieved in human life, so instead we should strive to persistently make progress. The goal is progress, not perfection.

Chapter 16:
Death Is Not the End

Our Ego Dies, Not Our Spirit

Human life does not last forever. Fortunately, most of us don't spend our entire lives thinking about the fact that we are going to die one day. However, at some point, most of us do deal with the loss of people and animals whom we care deeply about. Those times remind us of our own mortality. Physical death is inevitable.

We build tombs or try to leave legacies so that we are not "forgotten." Thinking about physical death, while not knowing or having faith in the truth about the greater eternal reality is sad and depressing. However, the spiritual part of us existed before our ego self, and will exist after our human life is over. It is an undisputed fact that our human bodies come and go.

But what happens to our limited conscious experience of memories as an individual here? I don't understand or claim to know exactly. I don't know if those parts of "us" are quarantined spiritually, and given another body to inhabit here, or given another life elsewhere, using the memories developed here in some way to evolve further in another state of amnesia. What I do know, because I was shown, is that all life on Earth is of a Greater Spirit of One. One source. I can say that all of us as a collective consciousness are shaping a Greater Spirit of One. I could guess that there are other dimensions, forms, expressions, hierarchies, and levels of the overall forever expanding and eternal thing called life, which comes from an origin of One.

Our human ego never wants to die. But our ego is just part of the temporary experience we have as human beings. In the big picture, we cannot see that everything will be alright. Really. The greater spiritual reality is better than you can imagine with a limited consciousness based on five senses. That's what my third revelation showed me. It is only my ego, the temporary part of me, that does not like the idea of an ending to my human existence of five senses. But when our human body dies, we are released from the five senses and become part of an unlimited consciousness again—that part of us that is eternal and One.

However, as a human being, you want to hear a more personal story. You want to hear about the eternal importance of your human identity establishing a deeper meaning into eternity. But that need is only based on human fear and ignorance. You don't know what you don't know. It's all going to be okay. It's all good.

Near-death experiences and deep meditation have one thing in common: the release, surrender, and detachment from the ego, or sense of self. It is a temporary release from the human experience with five senses. When people return from those experiences, they usually give accounts of perfect peace, which is the experience of our spiritual essence, the true greater reality, which is so beautiful that it is beyond verbal description. Our physical death is a release from limited consciousness into unlimited spiritual consciousness. Our spirit will always be a part of new life experiences into eternity.

Spiritual Death Does Not Exist

The death of self or our ego is actually a positive thing, but that's hard to grasp when it's all we "know" ourselves to be. Yes, ego comes and goes. It is born into a beginning, has a life experience with five senses, and then dies. To many people, the thought of surrendering to the end of life as we know it is troubling. The unknown is often frightening, but that's just our imaginations at work.

Some people believe that when we die we remain forever exactly as we are now. That's a human idea based on projection without an understanding of the greater reality beyond the one we experience with five senses. We imagine the afterlife this way because we don't want to let go of the loving connections we care about in this life. Our life with others has a unique meaning here, which we don't want to change or end. But at the moment of physical death, those worries and concerns end. There is no more separation, only total reunion with the Great Spirit of One—which spiritually includes everyone we have ever loved.

After physical death, we won't be in the same form, with a body, instincts, fears, limited senses, and ignorance of what we really are. The illusion of separateness is lifted upon physical death. There is no fear, only perfect peace.

Physical death is not terrifying. It's all good after this. It's all ours spiritually for eternity.

The Illusion of Separation

During my revelations, I received the ultimate gift. I was shown the greater unlimited reality beyond our five senses. That's the good news. The eternal part of us, our true life energy beyond our human shell and limited consciousness, goes on forever, living in infinite ways as part of the Greater Spirit of One, which the human brain cannot logically comprehend. Outside of this limited consciousness, there is unlimited spiritual consciousness, which is forever continuing and evolving as it wills.

I experienced a sequence of revelations: God is One; and God is not lonely, because it divided itself up into beings that live under the illusion that they are separate. God did this for the purpose of experiencing itself through interactions that would otherwise be unavailable. No matter what has happened in your human life experience, everything will be fine at the end of the ride. So, take a deep breath and relax. It's all good.

Fear Is Mostly Imagined

Remember this: we have a bad habit of exaggerating our fears, which almost never turn out to be as drastic as we imagine. There are the actual difficulties we have to deal with, and then there are the imaginary ones. Most of our hardships and worries are over imaginary fears that never happen. Remember that the next time you start freaking yourself out. Fear is a human ailment, with its only reason for existing being survival while you are in human form.

What Really Matters at the End of This Human Life?

If you ask people on their deathbeds what is most important to them, most will tell you that it is the meaningful connections they have made with others. What they gave to others, how they helped others is all that really matters in the end. What becomes meaningless is how much instinct-based sex they had for their own selfish gratification, or how much money they acquired for financial security that they can't take with them. All of the personal selfish experiences ultimately have no meaning. Love is the number one answer in the end. Love is all that matters—not the selfish love of self, but the unselfish loving of and from others. But what is love exactly? It is the primary eternal essence of what we are spiritually.

Chapter 17:
My Life Experiences with Grief and Miracles

My Experiences with Grief

If not processed and felt, grief will wait below the surface until it is experienced. Grief needs to be felt and processed completely in order for us to move past it. It can be delayed for some time, but it doesn't go away until it's processed.

There are five stages in processing grief, which occur in the following order:

- denial and isolation
- anger
- bargaining
- depression
- acceptance

My biggest challenges with grief began over ten years ago, when my dad died of heart failure. Then, six months later, my mom died unexpectedly on an Easter Sunday.

The last time I spoke with my mom was a week before her death. Due to an argument, the last thing I said to her was, "Don't call me anymore!" Then I hung up the phone. I was very sad at the time, because my mom had always been the warmest and most loving person I had ever known. But alcoholism took her away in the end. After her death, I withdrew into isolation. I remember feeling that my history had been erased somehow, with both my parents gone now. The two people who knew me and loved me most were gone. My life felt empty, like a ghost town, with its purpose and meaning now in question.

A few months after my mom's death, I became involved in a relationship with a woman I didn't get along with very well, but with whom I had passionate physical chemistry—not a good combination. I didn't have much to bring to the relationship, and was using it as a distraction to avoid my grief. But I remained in a deep depression, feeling numb most of the time, just going through the motions of life. Within a month of the beginning of that relationship, my partner became pregnant and had an abortion. A month later, she had a miscarriage, because it turned out that she had been pregnant with twins, and the doctors had been unaware of that when they performed the abortion. So, it was the second twin that miscarried. Thus, all within nine months, I experienced the abortion of my twins and the death of both of my parents.

During the two years of that relationship, there was a constant cloud of sadness in and around me. For those two years, I was isolated in the depression stage of grief. Then, when the relationship suddenly ended, I felt completely alone for the first time in my life. The grief that I had buried and avoided after the deaths of my dad, mom, and the aborted twins came rushing back and hit me all at once. I had sadness and grief on a level that completely devastated me for months. A constant, heavy, empty, dark feeling completely engulfed my daily life. In fact, the anxious pain became so severe that I actually passed out from it twice.

The grief was just waiting to be processed. Grief doesn't go away by avoiding it—it just waits to be felt and processed in the future. The two-year relationship had been a distraction for me to avoid feeling my grief and processing it. When you avoid and do not process grief, it hides under the surface as depression and waits.

Based on my own experiences, I would advise you, when you encounter loss and grief, to *feel* it. Don't try to avoid it. Experience it fully. Don't run from it. Move toward it and feel it. Grief is like an hourglass. When you flip it over and start experiencing the feelings, there is a limited amount of time to process the grief, and then it ends. But all the sand, all the grief, needs to drain out. The more you feel and process, the more you're putting behind you, and the more you won't need to feel that again in the future. Once you have totally processed the grief, you enter its final stage, which is acceptance.

Remember, feelings will never kill you. Move toward them, not away. Embrace them. Look at the pictures and listen to the songs that remind you of what makes you sad, and cry as much as you can. Crying drains the hourglass. Each minute of feeling grief takes you closer to acceptance, which is a place of no more pain. Each moment of feeling your pain brings you closer to being done with it and moving past it. Drain it completely. Do not avoid the feelings that hurt. Experience them as much as you can.

It's alright to be sad and cry. People are supposed to cry. The more we cry, the closer we come to ending the grieving process. We need to process the emotions so that we can get through the grief cycle, which ends in acceptance. If we don't process the grief, we stay stuck in denial, anger, and depression.

Grief follows the death of loved ones, the end of relationships, the loss of health, and the loss of financial security.

The Miracle Healing Story of My Dad's Pancreatic Cancer

Twenty years earlier, when I was 24 and going to college in Montana, I got the news that my dad had pancreatic cancer. He called me from Louisiana and said the doctors had told him he had only a month to live—one month. His attitude and personality had changed drastically since the last time I had spoken to him. He was no longer the stern, strict, critical man I had known all my life. Suddenly, he had become humble and kind. The barriers that had separated us before dropped away, and he talked to me as if I were an equal, a friend, for the first time ever.

Within days of getting the news about his diagnosis, my dad booked a plane to fly up to Montana to spend a week with me in my apartment. He met all my friends as we hung out. What an amazing time we had together, talking in a way that we had never talked before. Because we believed that he only had a month to live, we both made the time as special as we could.

After visiting me, my dad left to say goodbye to his friend "Mex," an old Navy buddy who lived in New Mexico. During that time with his friend, something very powerful and supernatural happened. When my dad first arrived, Mex told him, "Hey, we're going to take a trip in my car up to a place I want you to see. I wanna show you something." That was pretty much all he said, so my dad went along with it.

Mex drove my dad up to a place called El Santuario de Chimayó, a Roman Catholic church, located in the mountains

165

of Chimayó, New Mexico. The church has been there since the early 1800s. Nearby, there is a well in the ground, where the earth is dark red. Because the well is believed to contain "holy dirt," people who go there put a pinch of the dirt in their mouths, and then, inside the church, they ask God to heal them. In some cases, people have been healed instantly.

So, when my dad and Mex arrived there, my dad said, "What's this?"

They had driven for over an hour and a half, and now they were parked in front of a little church in the middle of nowhere up in the mountains of New Mexico.

Pointing toward the well, Mex said, "Get out, and go to that well over there. Get a pinch of the red dirt out of it, and put it in your mouth. Then go inside the church and ask God to heal you."

My dad's first reaction was to get mad.

"What the hell are you bringing me up here for?" he said. "I don't wanna do this. What are you doing? I'm not religious."

So, they argued for a bit, and then, since they were already there, my dad decided that he would go ahead and do what Mex had suggested. Still a little angry, he got out of the car, got a pinch of the red dirt from the well, put it in his mouth, and went inside the church, where he found that he was the only one inside. It was a small place, about the size of a 7-Eleven store, and there were crutches leaning against the walls on both sides, which had been left behind by people who had been healed there.

While standing inside the empty church, my dad decided to ask God to heal him.

"God," he said, "I haven't done what you wanted me to do much of the time, but I'd really like to live longer, and if it's your will, help me to live longer and heal me, please."

At that precise moment, he felt a sensation come into the top of his head and travel down from there throughout his entire body all the way to his feet. The sensation made him uncomfortable, as if he were hearing fingernails scratching on a chalkboard. That made him cringe and recoil, to the point that his knees buckled, causing him to fall to the ground. At that very moment, as was later confirmed by his doctors, the pancreatic cancer—a malignant tumor that had already taken over fifty percent of his pancreas—suddenly turned benign. The cancer was gone. He was healed.

My dad didn't know all that at that moment, but he knew something had happened because of the sensation that had made him fall to the ground. Was it something to do with the dirt? Was it a combination of eating the dirt and the prayer? Was it the location? It's a mystery. But the fact is that an inexplicable miracle did occur. My dad was instantly healed from an incurable disease.

A week later, after my dad returned home, he went to see his doctors. They ran all the cancer tests again, and this time everything came out normal. The tumor, which had been malignant, was now benign. The doctors had no medical explanation for this and were tongue-tied. None of his three doctors could explain it, other than to say it was a miracle.

"Yes," one of them said, "a miracle occurred. There's simply no other explanation, sir."

It seems that this should have been on the news, right? An actual miracle! But you know what? I didn't even believe this story myself until years later. When my dad first told it to me, I didn't believe it. I didn't believe it was God. And yet, dad's cancer had somehow been cured.

When dad first told me the story, he left out some details, so it wasn't until years later that he told me about the sensation in the top of his head, his knees going out, and his collapsing to the ground. After hearing those details, I believed the miracle had happened. I had to hear about the physical sensations for such an extraordinary experience to make logical sense to me. Sometimes the truth can be right in front of us, and we can still find a way not to see it. It's amazing how we can do that.

My dad ended up living another seventeen years after being instantly healed of pancreatic cancer. What a gift to be able to experience life for that much longer. He ultimately died of congestive heart failure. He's been gone for ten years now, but I have zero doubt that he experienced a true miraculous healing.

After that miraculous experience in New Mexico, my dad started going to a Catholic church, where he testified about what had happened to him. He loved talking to people, and he loved telling his story. He wanted to help people by inspiring them to go to the well. That was my dad's way of giving back: helping people to get healed.

Before he died, I asked him, "How many people do you think you sent to Chimayó who actually got healed? If you had to put a percentage on it, how many?"

He thought about that for a while, and finally said, "Probably around five percent."

One of the miraculous stories he told me was about a lady he knew from Baton Rouge, Louisiana, where he lived, and where I'm originally from. The lady, who came from a rich local family, had melanoma all over both arms, and her doctors said it was too far gone for them to be able to do anything about it. Huge spots of melanoma were spreading fast.

When my dad met her one day at church, and she shared her story with him, he told her to go to Chimayó. So, she went, and when she came back, my dad said, "She came running up my driveway and beating on my front door, yelling, 'Roy! Roy! Look—God healed me! Look! Look at my arms. Look!'"

Then she told my dad that when she went inside the church and asked God to heal her, the melanoma cancer spots instantly vanished, right in front of her eyes.

That's a hard one to believe, right? If I didn't come to believe in my dad's miracle, I probably wouldn't have believed hers.

It's hard for us to believe in miracles because we don't see many firsthand. Or if we do, we try to explain them away, automatically assuming that there must be some logical explanation that we don't know about.

I am telling this story to encourage people to go to the well at Chimayó, just as my dad did. Miracles do happen.

My Dad Contacts Me in a Dream

Three days after my dad died, I had a lucid dream—meaning I knew I was inside a dream as I was having it. In the dream, he called me on the phone to give me a message from the other side. His voice sounded peaceful, loving, and excited—not his normal serious tone. When I realized I was dreaming, I pulled the dream phone away from my ear and questioned whether any of this were real. Inside the dream, I asked myself, *Is this real? Wait, I know I'm in a dream.* Then I decided that it had to be real, so I put the dream phone back up to my ear to keep listening to what my dad was telling me from the other side.

Dad's primary message was to tell me, "It's all good."

He meant not to worry about this life or take it too seriously. In the end, he said, not to worry about his human death, or my own that was coming. Life continues.

Wow! Thanks, Dad, for letting me know that.

Then he ended the call with, "Hey, I have to go. But I wanted you to know that I love you, and I'm proud of you, and it's all good."

That dream was my second major "spiritual experience." After that call, I no longer grieved over his death. I knew now that he lived on in spirit. Of course, I was sad that he was gone from here, because I missed him. But I was more excited that he had contacted me to let me know that it's all good, and just to hang in there and do my best, without worrying and taking everything too seriously.

Chapter 18:
World Goals

In the "download" portion of my revelations, I received four goals for the world, which I discuss in detail below:

World Goal 1: Clean Drinking Water for Those Without It

Most of us live in our own bubble, ignoring as best we can the suffering all around us in the world. Out of sight, out of mind. We tend to believe that others' suffering does not affect us. However, we are all connected. Even if the suffering is on the other side of the planet, and we don't see or hear about it with our own eyes and ears, we still feel the pain of those who are suffering. Why? Because we are connected to it, since we are all really One spiritually beyond appearances. That is the truth.

We are not as separate as we appear to be, so shouldn't we be helping others who are outside our own bubbles? It is natural to not want to think about or focus on the suffering of others, which is depressing. If someone comes on TV to talk about starving people, most viewers will change the channel. We don't want to see that, or be swayed to feel any responsibility to help. Certainly, not after we just ate a great meal at a fancy restaurant.

I don't want to think about the fact that over six hundred million people throughout the world do not have access to clean drinking water. I don't want to contribute to solving the problem. I think, *Someone else will do it*, or *The problem is too big to solve, so any effort is useless*.

But as for the clean water issue, we currently have the means and the resources to bring relief in a relatively short period of time to most people in the world who lack access to clean drinking water. Nevertheless, as of yet, we have not done so.

It is absurd that people are suffering in this way right now when this problem could be solved fairly quickly with resources and technology that already exist. We could change the world in a big way right now if enough people give to the objective of everyone having access to clean drinking water. Go to *www.expertgiver. com* for links on how to help with this very important cause. One hundred percent of donations go toward solving this problem. All of the money donated goes straight to purchasing water wells and filtration in the most needy areas. I personally will profit in no way financially from this cause.

This is something we can do right now to help decrease suffering in the world. If enough of us donate a little, we can solve this problem. Imagine if you didn't have access to clean drinking water. Those of us who do have clean water are not thinking about the people who are suffering because they don't have it. We are selfish because we are ignorant. Whether we know it or not, the truth is that the suffering of others is also our suffering.

World Goal 2: Adopting Just One Homeless Person or Family

When I use the term *homeless*, I am not just referring to people who lack shelter. I am describing people who need extra help from others to get back to a place where their basic needs are met. Here is how to solve the homeless problem in the United States: Every capable individual will volunteer to support or sponsor one homeless person, one homeless couple, or one homeless family with kids. That involves doing whatever it takes to get those people on their feet, with money, clothing, shelter, food, work, and medical and mental health resources. This will require giving, even when that is not convenient.

Can you help just one person come up from the bottom?

Judging the Homeless in Five Seconds

When you are driving and see a lost dog with a collar wandering around, do you pull over and try to call it to you so you can check the collar and call the owner? Or do you just keep driving and think, *Someone else will do it*?

Most of the time, you are probably more willing to help a lost animal than a needy human. Is that because you think the animal is helpless, whereas humans are not? How is it that you will adopt abused animals, but you won't adopt homeless people, helping them with your time, attention, and resources to get back on track?

When you see homeless people on a street corner, do you think: *They don't deserve anything from me. I don't want to enable them. If I give them money, it's going to keep them on this corner. I don't want to pay for them to just sit here, so I have to look at them tomorrow and feel uncomfortable again for not helping. I'm doing a public service by not helping them. How dare they beg and make me feel uncomfortable? They must be junkies or lazy, and they're just scamming others by pretending to be homeless because they don't want to work and earn a living like me. Their problem is that they don't want to grow up—they just want others to take care of them. I'm earning what I have! Get a job and take care of yourself, the way I do!"*

That's what our brains do—that's what our selfish instincts tell us. Instead, how about thinking, *I have no idea what their story is, but I can see that their fingernails are dirty, and I can see that they are out there in the elements, and I can see that they are asking for help. I can see that they are struggling to meet their own basic needs. I can see that maybe they forgot how to be givers, or just never learned how they could contribute to others in a positive way. I can see that they appear to just be taking, not giving. Yes, I can see all of that, but unless I spend some time talking to them, do I know through judgment in a single moment the real reason for their circumstances? Do I know their history, their pain, and their struggles? Am I willing to pull over and talk to them to find out?*

Wait! Does everyone have to deserve my help for me to give it? How about I just help in some way—regardless of whether those homeless people deserve it?

Pity the poor homeless because, in many cases, their stories are totally different from what you think. Those stories are never as black-and-white as your judgment determines, based on briefly observing the poor characters' external appearance. I usually judge them quickly with a glance, justifying why I shouldn't help them without talking to them to hear their story. The real story is usually different from what I imagine, as I will discover if I take the time to actually talk to them.

The point is, regardless of the reason for their being homeless or begging, many of them do need our help. We tell ourselves that other people are helping, or will help, so we don't have to. That is an excuse to shift responsibility to others, allowing us to neglect the homeless and their suffering. Many people who need help are not getting it—at least, not the real consistent help that requires time, patience, energy, and follow-through.

Just giving poor people money is treating the symptom and not the problem. It is guilty quick-fix help, which is ineffective. Those poor folks need a longer-term commitment of help. They need more than a few minutes of your time. There are many reasons why people are incapable of taking care of their own basic needs, including drug or alcohol addiction, a decline in health, loss of loved ones, job loss, or mental illness with no help from family members. If you ask them their story, they will reveal their struggles fairly quickly.

When you help the homeless, you may get your hands dirty, and it may take several attempts to find someone you can help, since some people don't want to be helped.

Four Categories of Homeless People

Again, when I use the term *homeless*, I am referring to more than just the people you see on the side of the road, packing their belongings. I am also referring to people who may have a place to sleep, but who are alone, neglected, and don't have other people helping them out. So when I use the term homeless, I am also referring to people who need help from others getting to a place where they, too, can start helping others.

I have come up with four categories of homeless people who need our help. Let's examine each.

The first category is *people with drug addiction*. Some have lost the ability to take care of themselves due to their addiction.

However, giving those people money is not the solution. But feeding them is something you can do, and while you are doing that, you can give them time, attention, and words of encouragement. You can also help them get into a detox or treatment facility. Another way to help addicts is to offer to take them to an AA group to meet others who can better help them with their problem. Most of the time, giving them money directly only enables them to continue their addiction.

The second type of homeless people are those who are *mentally ill*. Schizophrenia is common among this group, as well as various post-traumatic stress disorders. Many members of this group are veterans and victims of abuse. Many cannot hold jobs or provide for their own basic needs, including food and shelter. Some mentally ill people have no family members to support or help them, and some have families that have rejected them, so they end up on the streets. My own sister is schizophrenic, so I know from experience that dealing with mental illness can be very challenging.

Some mentally ill people reject help. And many of them don't have the capacity to get help for themselves. They need help from others to provide for their basic needs. Many of them need sustained help, which requires patience and tolerance. They may need help researching and locating resources to help themselves. That will require giving of your time and effort. For example, you might take them to a Department of Social and Health Services (DSHS) office, where they can apply for resources such as housing assistance, food stamps, and medical assistance.

There is an application for long-term care available at DSHS offices, which is the first step in applying for long-term help for disabled or mentally ill people who cannot help themselves. That involves setting up an appointment with a social worker to discuss the individual's specific needs and issues. You may allow the individual to use your address and phone number to assist with his or her applications, and then follow up with them, meeting them at or taking them to their appointments in these critical first steps of getting the help they need.

The third type of homeless people are those who have *experienced financial hardship* that led to their homelessness. They may have lost the ability to provide basic food and shelter for themselves for a variety of reasons, including job loss, a decline in health, grief over losing a loved one, or extreme stress and anxiety from traumatic experiences. Many of these reasons are beyond their immediate control. But regardless of the reasons, they need help and guidance with taking care of themselves. Some people find themselves alone in the world, with no one there to help them out.

The fourth type of homeless people are those who *choose homelessness as an actual occupation*, in which they beg from others to meet their basic needs. Some of these people do not want to change. However, if some of these homeless individuals were to show an interest in going to an Expert Giver Group meeting and decided to work through the steps voluntarily, they could grow away from total dependency on others' giving, and transform their lives into contributing and giving to others. We don't try to force or persuade these individuals to transform themselves, but we do help those who want our help. Find one person who truly wants and needs the help you are offering. There will be no greater reward than helping to lift another person up to make the transition from taker to giver.

Once you have found one homeless person who wants and

needs your help, it is up to you to follow through, continue leading the plan in helping him (or her), and continue helping him as long as he is doing what is required to help himself along the way. We can each choose to sponsor one homeless person, one homeless couple, or one homeless family. We can teach them how to give through our example, and give to them unconditionally until they learn to give unconditionally themselves—whether we help them financially, by giving of our time, or by being kind and patient.

Where do you find homeless people? At food banks, in homeless camps, or on the streets. You can also find them in churches or Salvation Army centers. The homeless individual may have lost a job, or have health problems, or have spiraled down into depression from the loss of a relationship or a family member, and he can't pull out of grief. Or he may be alone in the world without any family, and no one who cares about him.

To practice giving with individuals you see on the street, approach them directly. Then smile and ask, "How are you doing with life right now? Tell me about it." Then wait for their answer and respond lovingly, as you would want someone to do with you if you were in their shoes. They will probably start by talking about their finances and ask if you can spare some change. How would you want someone to ask *you* about your life, and talk to you, and treat you, and try to help you if you were on the streets? That is exactly what you should do with people you decide to help. You listen to their story, which will contain fear and possible delusions, or a con line to get money, but know that, deep down inside, they want to give again. They want to earn everything they get by giving, but they have either forgotten how or they never learned how to practice giving.

Instead of giving them money, ask them if they would like to join you for a meal, so you can interact with them and get them to open up more about what is really going on in their lives. Find out their situation, beyond their sales pitch to get your money. Many of them are in survival mode and have concocted lies about their situation. They aren't used to people spending time talking to them or willing to help them in a sustained effort.

You need to take time to get their real story. If you are willing to spend thirty to forty-five minutes with them and get beyond their "ask" and their lies to get money, you may find individuals who could use your help beyond a couple of dollars and a hurried smile. Drive them somewhere or walk with them and feed them. Discuss their situation over a meal or at a coffee shop. However, use caution so that you don't put yourself in harmful or dangerous situations.

Help them to figure out what they can do to help themselves, and how you can best assist them so that they can give again, too. Get their phone number, if they have one, so you can follow up with them. If they don't have a phone, set a time and place to meet again. Make a plan based on their needs, with specific goals to follow up on. Then plan the next meeting. If all this doesn't turn out the way you hoped, just ask them if they are hungry. Then feed them.

Let them know up front that you are not offering a source of income or future money, but will help with time and energy. Treat them as you would want to be treated if you were in the same circumstances.

Expert Giver Groups can offer support with helping the homeless. For more information, check out *www.ExpertGiver.com*.

World Goal 3: Getting Rid of Nuclear Weapons

Another world goal that I was given in my revelation "down-load" was to suggest visualizing world peace for one full minute, every day, upon awakening. This may sound kooky. But it will work if enough of us do it persistently.

Your imagination is powerful. If you imagine something enough times, and with focused attention, the wheels start grinding behind the scenes to materialize it in this world. This is how we can produce something from nothing. Every man-made object in this world was first imagined at one point, and then desired. I know that *materialize* is a New-Age word, but we each have this superpower.

To practice using your imagination with the intent of creating and manifesting what you want, start by holding the picture of what you desire in your mind and attempt to have the feelings that would come from having it, as if it has already happened. When you focus a desire and believe in it persistently without doubt, you can materialize that desire.

Although you have done nothing outside your mind's desire, powerful unseen forces are starting to churn to bring your desire about. You cannot see exactly how the pieces will come together, but imagining the outcome with desire is all you need to do to start the process of materializing it in the physical world.

Over a decade ago, there was a popular book called *The Secret*, which explained that if you can repeatedly imagine a desired out-come as already existing, and repeat this exercise, it will come to be over time. The overall problem with *The Secret* was that it promoted using this power for selfish reasons, to gain material things and wealth. It was all about using this power for getting, and not for giving. The solution here is not to feed our instincts' insatiable desire for sex, financial security, and selfish fulfillment. The solution is giving.

If enough people in the world decided to visualize nuclear disarmament for one minute a day, that would manifest in reality over time. Our collective intent is humanity's most powerful tool, which most of us don't realize we have. We can remove all nuclear weapons from the world if enough of us desire it, will it to be so, and persistently visualize it. I cannot explain this power, but it will work if enough of us use it.

I was on Google recently, checking the news, and the first article I saw said, "Doomsday Clock Moves Closer to Midnight."

Nuclear war. Wow. It has moved closer, especially with the tensions between India and Pakistan, which can affect the whole world. But we can stop it from happening. However, it will require a little action on all our parts. Will you commit to one minute per day? A simple visualization, lasting one minute per day, with the intent and desire to eradicate nuclear weapons, could cause an actual reduction of them in the world if enough people choose to do this practice. All I'm asking of you is *one minute per day* when you wake up.

If enough of us practice the daily nuclear reduction visualization, then a process of actual nuclear reduction will start to occur. However, enough of us need to do it to reach the critical mass threshold that triggers the huge wheels behind the scenes to start to clank and turn. Can we change the world? Yes, with enough concentrated intentions consistently practiced over time. But it is a commitment that enough of us need to make repeatedly until the desired results are attained. Commitment, persistence, and action are required from a large number of us. Enough of us have to want it—not just *say* we want it. Enough of us have to concentrate on wanting it every day.

Will you join me in this exercise of focusing on having no more nuclear bombs in the world, and being a part of manifesting that? Imagine all the nations of the world dismantling and eradicating their nukes. Visualize people around the planet hugging one another and crying with joy over this accomplishment.

This is quantum physics stuff, so it doesn't make logical sense. But we actually have that power and ability when effort and belief are applied consistently. To be effective at creating and manifesting, we must keep up a concentrated, persistent effort over time, despite all the distractions of life. Persistence requires discipline, but it pays off. Everyone who has achieved anything of value in this world has demonstrated persistence. In the face of difficulty, they remained steady in the pursuit of their goal, whatever it was. Let's use persistent intention to manifest peace in the world, and make something big happen that is good for everyone.

World Goal 4: Population Reduction

The number one problem in the world right now, the biggest elephant in the room, is overpopulation. We cannot control our own instincts to stop it, limit it, or reverse it. We are in a state of denial about it. Right now, we have 7.6 billion people on Earth. Our instincts tell us to keep having more kids. A woman's most basic primal urge is to become pregnant and have a baby. Most women want to do that more than any other single thing in their lives. And men want to impregnate women as a powerful instinctual and hormonal drive. The most fundamental drive in both men and women is to procreate.

For the survival of our species, we really need to reduce the exponential production of more of us. I am suggesting that not producing more kids is an act of giving. Please consider adoption. It is a sacrifice, but unconditional giving requires sacrifice. For the greater good, we must sacrifice in order to continue our survival. Our current population trajectory is unsustainable. Every day, 200,000 new people are added to the population—or 1,000,000 new people every five days. These numbers take into account how many people die daily. Think about those numbers. Birth control and sterilization are some commonsense options.

Choosing to go against our strongest instinctual drives to procreate is unconditional giving, and also a sacrifice for our own greater good.

Exponential population growth is unsustainable, but our denial says otherwise. We are rushing toward a trip-wire threshold in our world of limited resources. There are not enough resources for everyone to consume at the standard of the modern world. Can you be part of the solution?

Chapter 19:
Expert Giver Groups

Introduction

Shortly after my revelations, the term *Expert Giver* came up in my mind. I went online in January 2018 to search for the domain name *ExpertGiver.com*, and discovered that it was available to purchase for ten dollars. What are the odds of that domain being available at that time for that price? All of the information contained in this book concerning the chapters on World Goals and Expert Giver Groups will be provided free on the website.

We are becoming more and more divided, separated, and isolated from each other. Many of us do not have the kind of genuine connections that we all long for. We want to connect, but don't know how, or where to do it. My intent for the Expert Giver Groups is to provide a new way for people to connect directly in person to build meaningful supportive relationships around the principles of humility, accountability, forgiveness, and unconditional giving. And it won't be corrupted by money. There will be no fees or dues for membership. Expert Giver Groups are open to all people, regardless of age, race, culture, sexuality, socioeconomic status, religion, or political affiliation.

Check out: *www.ExpertGiver.com*. Join or start a group today.

The Foundation of Expert Giver Groups Comes from AA's Proven Methods

You may or may not be familiar with Alcoholics Anonymous (AA), which was started in the 1930s by a stockbroker named Bill Wilson. If you aren't familiar with the AA program, you may guess that it is about people sitting around in groups, discussing how to stop drinking, and that's it. But the program is much deeper than most people know. When I was 15, I got my first girlfriend. She told me, "You should go to Alcoholics Anonymous and stop hanging around your friends who drink." So I did. AA was the first place I witnessed people helping each other without selfish motives. I am grateful for my experience with the AA program, and for the influence it has had on my life.

AA has twelve steps, which I won't go through in detail, but they provide methods that convert people from takers to givers. The steps involve personal inventory, accountability, forgiveness, and service to others. I have taken the fundamental core elements that have proven to work in AA, and created the Seven Steps of Expert Giver Groups.

In this book, I talk about "God." But in the Seven Steps of Expert Giver Groups, I don't mention "God" or a "Higher Power." That concept is for all individuals to determine for themselves, whether or not they follow a particular religion. My intent is for the Seven Steps of Expert Giver Groups to provide the tools needed to remove the blocks in the way of individuals becoming of service to others, which will lead to their spiritual awakening. My wish is that Expert Giver Groups will remain free from arguments over religion or politics. Functional unity is paramount.

The 7 Steps of Expert Giver Groups (Short Form)

Step 1: Finding a Mentor in an Expert Giver Group.
Admit that you need help managing your instinctual drives, and are willing to become humble and teachable, and to seek humility by finding a mentor in an Expert Giver Group and by committing to being honest and accountable to that person.

Step 2: Completing Your Personal Inventories. In the formats suggested, write down four different personal inventories: (a) Resentments; (b) Relationships; (c) Fears; and (d) Character Defects.

Step 3: Reviewing All Four of Your Inventories with Your Mentor. Once you complete all four inventories in Step 2, arrange a meeting with your mentor to humbly and honestly go over all the lists together, being open to feedback that helps you to see things that you could not see on your own.

Step 4: Making a List of Amends and Reviewing It with Your Mentor. Make a list of amends that you owe to others, and review the list with your mentor.

Step 5: Making Your Amends. After you review with your mentor which amends to make and how to make them, start making those amends.

Step 6: Continue Taking Your Personal Inventory and Promptly Admit When You Are Wrong. Continue reviewing your resentments, intimate relationships, fears, and character defects—promptly admitting when you are wrong, and making amends immediately when you cause harm to others.

Step 7: Mentoring Others. Offer to become a mentor for others who are willing to go through the above steps. Be as unconditionally giving as you can in service to others. Be open to starting an Expert Giver Group in your area.

The 7 Steps of Expert Giver Groups (Long Form)

Step 1: Finding a Mentor in an Expert Giver Group

Admit that you need help managing your instinctual drives, and are willing to become humble and teachable, and to seek humility by finding a mentor in an Expert Giver Group and by committing to being honest and accountable to that person.

Humility **defined:**
- A modest or low view of one's own importance; humbleness.

Humiliate **defined:**
- To make someone feel ashamed and foolish by injuring his or her dignity and self-respect, especially publicly.

Humility requires a modest or low view of your own importance. To be humble is to admit that you don't have all the answers, and so are teachable and open-minded.

Some people mock humility or put it down as if it were a weakness, but that comes from denial or ignorance. Humility is required for honest self-examination. Humility is required to become accountable to others, allowing them to give you constructive criticism so that you may advance in your giving and service to others. Humility is saying, "I don't know it all," and then being open to constructive feedback from others to examine how we can improve.

The reality is, you can't always trust your own thoughts and ideas, because they are driven by your instinctual drives, which can cause you to justify selfish behaviors, which in turn can result in neglect or harm to yourself or others. Because of your instinctual drives, you can justify why it is alright to be selfish or to harm others, directly or indirectly. Having humility means allowing feedback, suggestions, and constructive criticism from other people who want to help you grow. When you have ideas that may be selfish, practicing humility requires you to "tell on yourself" to others to whom you are accountable.

Like an adolescent child, the ego says, "I know it all, and I decide everything for myself." The ego does not like to examine its faults or to practice humility. It prefers to justify its faults or blame others for them.

The humble person responds, "The greater good is important. I don't have all the answers, and before taking a questionable action, I will check myself by being accountable to my motives, and I will bounce this off my mentor or a close friend who cares about me and wants the best for me."

Some people do not have good friends or mentors in their lives who can help them in this way, or who have their best interests at heart. Many people do not have access to other people who really care about them, want to see them succeed, and get better. Many people get together and validate the selfish instinctual behaviors of their egos with each other. Relationships of this nature are empty and unsatisfying. Ideally, both parties in a relationship should have a genuine desire to support each other in encouraging service, unconditional giving, and forgiveness toward others. We need to become examples and coaches for each other to encourage these qualities. But there are not many places to go that give us the tools and methods that enable us to start interacting with these intentions.

Humility is not the same as humiliation, which is the act of being dishonored, disgraced, embarrassed, and shamed. When you see a big ego getting humiliated, you love it, because privately you want that person to be taught a lesson and get put in his or her place. You want to see egotistical people become humble because you don't really appreciate, respect, or admire inflated egos. Humiliation is painful, because it is meant to direct a person toward humility. It is the discipline needed to correct egotistical behavior. None of us like discipline or being corrected, especially when we are being selfish. A humble person, when confronted about being selfish, will simply say, "Yeah, you're right. Thanks for helping me to see that. Forgive me. I'll try to do that differently next time."

Some people pretend to admire others who have a big ego when, deep down, they don't really like them. No one likes people who brag about themselves, are selfish, and claim to know everything. But we do appreciate, respect, and admire humility. We admire humble men and women who don't take selfish shortcuts that hurt others. Humble people can admit when they are wrong. Humble people are not victims who blame others. Humble people are the ones we respect and admire the most. They are the examples that we all need and want. Humility is true strength, not weakness. What are *you* teaching others by your example?

Self-centeredness, driven by our instincts, hormones, and the illusion of separation, is the root of our problems. Self-centeredness directs us to self-focus, seeking self-gratification, pleasure, sex, and excessive money. Sometimes we justify hurting others in the process of satisfying our selfish motives.

The selfish instinctual drives are not inherently bad or sinful.

They are natural and human, but become bad and sinful when they control us and dominate us, demanding more than is necessary, and causing us to justify selfishly hurting ourselves and others. The ultimate goal is to live without our instincts causing harm to ourselves or others. We need help with instinct management, and we can't do it alone. Humility is required to get the ongoing help and support we need from others.

Finding a mentor who can give you feedback is the first step toward gaining humility. Having a mentor will be helpful in checking whether your choices are to serve or to be selfish—that is, if your motives come from the heart or from self-centered instinctual drives. The latter can dominate and blind you quickly if they are left unchecked and under your own stewardship. Alone you lose. Together you win. Helping you is helping me.

Willingness to acquire humility is the only requirement for membership in Expert Giver Groups. Humility is required to take accountability and responsibility for our own lives. Humility is very rare in today's world because most people operate from an "I'm right, and you're wrong" perspective. The blame game is default human behavior. "It's your fault. I didn't do it." People don't like to admit how they're wrong. Many of us point the finger of blame at other people for our problems and circumstances. We often seek to divert attention away from ourselves when we were wrong— because the last thing we want to do is say, "I'm sorry," or "I was wrong about that," or "Please forgive me, I just didn't know."

If you are your own mentor, your pride, ego, and instincts will not allow you to see and admit when you are wrong. That would require you to examine your selfish motives before you act. The process of accountability to another person requires humility, which is an admission that you need help from others.

However, many of us have been hurt over and over again by different people throughout our lives. We have all been let down, tricked, conned, and scammed. Because of that, we have given up hope in the goodness of others, and in their ability to be trustworthy with our best interests at heart. With the increasing fear of others and the lack of trust that most of us have, we don't want to be vulnerable, or to take the risk of being used or hurt by another's selfish motives. Therefore, we have become more and more isolated. Many people believe that the idea of others helping them with pure motives is impossible. But being open to trusting again is required in order to develop a productive relationship with a mentor.

We have lost trust in each other's motives. But to change and grow, we need honest feedback from each other, which involves trust. When people first go to an Expert Giver Group meeting, they are received with open arms, and they experience other people who just want to help them get better. At first, the newcomers may not trust that the help is without selfish motives. They may think, *What's the catch here?* But after a short time, they will realize that there *is* no catch. Then they begin to truly appreciate the fact that most people there have good intentions to truly help each other grow and succeed, without hidden motives for sex or money. How much do we experience this in the real world? Sadly, not much. My goal with the Expert Giver Groups is to connect people with the goal of unconditionally helping each other with no hidden motives and no strings attached.

I suggest that you choose a mentor from an Expert Giver meeting. This will be someone who wants to help you grow, and who is committed to doing so. I do not recommend having people of the opposite gender mentoring each other because of the possibility of sexual motives entering the picture. But this is only a recommendation, not a rule. The mentor is there to help you go through the Seven Steps, to develop an accountability feedback relationship, and to share experience, strength, and hope.

Your mentor's goal is to have a sincere desire to help you without seeking anything in return. Follow your gut and your intuition. It is okay to change mentors. I recommend getting a mentor within your first few Expert Giver meetings. At least, choose a temporary mentor and exchange numbers within the first two meetings. The first step is to become accountable to another person. I recommend daily phone contact for the first month, and weekly in-person meetings of at least an hour, if possible. A mentor will be your guide through the remaining steps below.

Are you teachable? Acquiring humility combined with open-mindedness, willingness, and honesty are the keys to begin managing your instinctual drives, to start your transition from a taker to an Expert Giver.

Step 2: Completing Your Personal Inventories

In the formats suggested below, write down four different personal inventories: Resentments; Intimate Relationships; Fears; and Character Defects.

I recommend keeping your inventories private from others. They will be only for you and your mentor to review together, after which you may choose to dispose of them or save them for review later.

There will never be a perfect time to begin writing out the lists below. You just need to start. Once you begin writing, it will start flowing. I found that I got most of it done in a couple of sittings over several hours. But everyone will be different about the time required. The first time you have thirty minutes to dedicate to it, do it. Don't put it off. It's important. Completing these inventories will be life-changing.

Resentment defined:
- *Bitter indignation at having been treated unfairly.*

List Your Resentments. In the following sections, you will be creating four resentment lists, which you will ultimately combine into one master list that will look like Table 1, below:

Table 1: Master List of Resentments

Resentment List #1 (Offenders)	Resentment List #2: What Happened / Instincts Affected	Resentment List #3: My Part	Resentment List #4: Forgiveness (when I have no part)
Boss from XYZ, Inc.	Fired me from my job at XYZ / *Security (emotional and financial)*	I did poor work; I showed up late for work too many times	—
Wife	Cheated on me with my friend / *Sex; Security (emotional)*	I was not emotionally available; I cheated on her a year earlier	—
Male Mugger	Threatened me with a gun and stole my wallet / *Security (personal, emotional, and financial)*	I had no part	I forgive him
Female Co-worker	Insulted me / *Security (emotional)*	I insulted her three weeks earlier	—
Etc.			

Resentment List #1: Name All of Your Resentments by Offenders. Either by hand or with a computer spreadsheet, create a four-column list as in Figure 2, above. Label the first column, "Resentment List #1 (Offenders)." Then list all the people and institutions that you still feel angry toward—*everyone* you hold a grudge against, in any order you think of them. This list might contain family members, friends, previous bosses, policemen, judges, teachers, bullies, institutions, politicians, former romantic partners, and so on.

Table 2, below, shows an example of Resentment List #1:

Table 2: Resentment List #1 (Offenders)

Boss from XYZ, Inc.
Wife
Male Mugger
Female Co-worker
Etc.

Resentment List #2: Name All of Your Resentments by What Happened and the Instincts Affected. Label the second column, "Resentment List #2 (What Happened / Instincts Affected)." Then describe exactly what happened that made you upset. If there is more than one offense to list under that person or organization, write them all down.

How did the person or organization wrong you? What did they do to hurt you or make you angry? Does what he or she did affect your instincts for sex or security? Throughout this book, I have mostly referred to security as it relates to money. However, as we noted earlier, in addition to financial security, there are also personal and emotional security. When we examine our resentments and which instincts are affected by them, it may be our personal or emotional security that was affected instead of our financial security. So as you are labeling which instincts are affected, security can be thought of as money, physical health and safety, or emotional/social well-being.

Some examples of your *financial security* being affected might include: (1) someone took away your income or job; (2) someone stopped providing for you; or (3) someone set a boundary that cut off your resources.

Some examples of your *personal security* being affected might be: (1) someone harmed you physically; (2) someone threatened to harm you physically; or (3) someone deprived you of food and shelter.

Some examples of your *emotional security* being affected might be: (1) someone hurt your feelings; (2) someone abandoned you; or (3) someone interfered with an important relationship in your life.

Some examples of your *sex instinct* being affected might include: (1) someone cheated on you sexually; (2) someone stopped providing sex for you; or (3) someone shamed you about your sexual desires or orientation.

Table 3, below, shows an example of Resentment List #2:

Table 3: Resentment List #2
(What Happened / Instincts Affected)

Boss fired me from my job at XYZ / *Security (emotional and financial)*
Wife cheated on me with my friend / *Sex; Security (emotional)*
Mugger stole my wallet at gunpoint / *Security (personal, emotional, and financial)*
Female co-worker insulted me / *Security (emotional)*
Etc.

This second list will reveal all the blocks that keep you poisoned with anger and resentment. Resentments are poisons that are hurting *you*, not the people or institutions that you feel angry toward.

You have now listed all the people who have harmed you or whom you are mad at; you have listed exactly what happened; and you have listed whether the action threatened your instincts concerning sex or security. When you are done with List #2, you are now ready to determine if you played a part in any of your resentments.

List #3: Determining Your Part in Each Resentment. The third part of your resentment inventory is to describe in writing *your* part in creating or causing your resentments. To make this third list, for each offender write down your part in causing the person to react negatively to you.

196

Was the other party reacting to or retaliating for something you did? People often do things that hurt us because we stepped on their toes in some way, or we had some part to play in causing their reaction. But many times, we are unaware of the part that we played. When we think about it, we usually find that we have blamed others for retaliating for something that *we* started in the first place. In the *My Part* list, you take responsibility for your own actions. The task of finding and admitting your part is about reviewing *your* fault, not the other person's fault. This exercise is about looking at yourself, not others.

What is your part, and where are you to blame? This shifts your perspective from nurturing a victim mentality to owning up to how you played a part, taking responsibility for the role you played. That requires honesty, humility, and courage to examine your part for the first time. It is not easy to look at your own part, or to admit what you did that caused another person to harm you. Most people only focus on the other person, ignore their own part, and justify being a victim. It's natural for us to blame others; that's our default mode. It takes courage and humility to look at and acknowledge our own part honestly. That is the beginning of the truth setting you free.

On your third list, here are some questions to help you examine if you played a part in your resentments. You don't need to write out all the questions. Just use them as guidelines to uncover your role in reviewing your part, if any, in what happened.

- Was I taking advantage of others, using them, or expecting more than I should have from them?
- Did I make demands or set expectations for them that they did not agree to fulfill?

- Did they set a boundary or limit that I didn't like, and so I reacted in anger?
- What did I do to them first for them to react this way?
- Did I threaten their instincts for sex or security?
- Did they threaten *my* instincts for sex or security?
- Did I lie, cheat, or steal?
- What could I have done differently?

Even if other people deserve some portion of the blame, this inventory is not about them—it is about examining *your* part in how *you* caused people to react against you—in other words, you discover your own part in causing your resentment.

Table 4, below, shows an example of Resentment List #3:

Table 4: Resentment List #3
(My Part in What Happened)

Boss: I did poor work; I showed up late for work too many times
Wife: I was not emotionally available; I cheated on her a year earlier
Male Mugger: I had no part
Female Co-worker: I insulted her three weeks earlier
Etc.

List #4: Practicing Forgiveness of Resentments in Which You Played No Part. What about when, as with the Male Mugger above, you have *no* part in your resentment? Sometimes sick, ignorant, or criminal people harm us for no reason caused by us, but still they hurt us. In some instances, we are truly the victim of another's selfish, harmful actions. How do we deal with resentments that we haven't caused? The answer may initially seem impossible. But the resentment that you feel only hurts *you*.

Forgiveness goes against your feelings of "justified" resentment. However, ultimately, forgiveness is the solution, because the forgiveness is really for you and your freedom from the resentment. To forgive despite your "justified" anger is no easy task. But resentments are the number one block that hold us back from unconditional giving to and serving of others. To be truly free, you must forgive the other party—but it is a hard choice to make.

Table 5, below, shows an example of Resentment List #4:

Table 5: Resentment List #4
(Forgiveness, when I have no part)

Boss: —
Wife: —
Male Mugger: I forgive him
Female Co-worker: —
Etc.

So, how do you practice forgiveness? At times when you are alone, I suggest that you say out loud, "I forgive 'so-and-so' for doing 'such-and-such' because he or she is a sick, ignorant, or criminal person operating from his or her instincts. I hope that 'so-and-so' figures out how to become giving in this life, so he or she can have all the happiness, peace, joy, and wisdom available to a human being." I would suggest doing this every day until the resentment is gone, and you have totally forgiven the other person.

It's not easy, but it has worked for me, taking anywhere from one to three weeks. Forgiveness is the biggest give, and it is required for you to heal and be free.

Now that you have completed all four sections of your Resentment Inventory (Offenders; What Happened / Instincts Affected; My Part; and Forgiveness), you are ready to begin your Intimate Relationship Inventory.

List Your Intimate Relationships. Make a list of *all* the people with whom you have had previous intimate relations, using their first name or initials. The purpose here is *not* to describe or discuss details of how and what we have done sexually, or our sexual tastes and preferences. To that I say, "To each his own."

Create a list of all your previous intimate partners. As you list each name, write out the answers to each question below:

- **Selfishness:** How was I ever selfish?
- **Dishonesty:** How was I ever dishonest?
- **Inconsideration:** How was I ever inconsiderate?
- **Jealousy:** How did I ever create jealousy?
- **Alternative Behavior:** What could I have done differently?

Examples:

Pam (my ex-wife):

Selfishness: I only took care of my own selfish sexual desires.

Dishonesty: I cheated on Pam with Susan.

Inconsideration: I disregarded Pam's feelings.

Jealousy: Pam found out and became jealous.

Alternative Behavior: I should have divorced Pam or separated from her before seeing other women.

Susan:

Selfishness: I put my own interests before hers.

Dishonesty: I lied about being single so I could have sex with her.

Inconsideration: I disregarded Susan's feelings.

Jealousy: n/a: Susan never found out about Pam.

Alternative Behavior: I should have divorced Pam or separated from her before seeing Susan.

Monica:

Selfishness: I put my own interests before hers.

Dishonesty: I told her I loved her when I didn't mean it so she would stay with me because I wanted the companionship and didn't want to be alone.

Inconsideration: I ignored Monica's feelings.

Jealousy: n/a
Alternative Behavior: I should have told Monica the truth, regardless of the consequences.

Kim:

Selfishness: While in a relationship with Kim, I spent time with other female friends I was attracted to sexually because I wanted to find another partner before ending the relationship with Kim.

Dishonesty: I lied to Kim about seeing other women.

Inconsideration: I disregarded Kim's feelings.

Jealousy: Kim would have become jealous if she ever found out about the other women, which she did not.

Alternative Behavior: I should have separated from Kim before looking for other women to date.

List Your Fears. Fear is defined as "an unpleasant emotion caused by the belief that someone or something is dangerous and likely to cause us pain or threat." Fear is based on the belief that we will lose something that we already possess, or won't get something that we want, need, or demand. Fears are based on our survival instincts, for they help to keep us alive. But they are also the primary cause of our self-centeredness. Human beings have a complex design, which inclines us to be suspicious and not immediately trust other people. We are on guard against being hurt, conned, or tricked. The world is selfish, so fear drives everyone to varying degrees.

When our basic needs for food, shelter, and sex are met, we experience little stress and fear, which allows us to become more giving toward others. Our instincts create the fears that drive our insecurities of not having enough—primarily not having enough financial, personal, or emotional security. The drives of our fears and instincts tell us that "more" will fulfill us—but "satisfaction" is never obtained. We can get stuck living in a constant state of fear and lack, which then converts excess wants into needs that can never be satisfied, no matter how much we obtain. We do need some level of selfishness to survive, but once our basic needs are met, most of us still want "more." Just when we should be slowing down for the stop sign, our instinctual drives, fueled by fear, reach down and push the gas pedal all the way to the floor.

Write down a numbered list of all your fears, and relate them to the instinct affected:

1. Fear of losing my job. (Financial, Personal, and Emotional Security)
2. Fear of losing my intimate partner. (Sex & Emotional Security)
3. Fear of losing my house. (Financial, Personal, and Emotional Security)
4. Fear of dying from cancer (Personal and Emotional Security)
5. Etc.

List Your Character Defects. Our main character defects are based on fear and self-centeredness. Write out how the character defects below appear in your life today, so you can become aware of how they block your ability to give. Ask yourself how the following thoughts do or do not apply to you:

1. Greed: I don't have enough to share with others, and I always need *more* to be okay. It doesn't matter how much I accumulate. No matter how much I have, I am always dissatisfied, so I justify being selfish, wanting more, and needing to keep more for myself. My goal is to always be as generous as possible. *List examples of my being greedy, writing down the who and the why.*

2. Jealousy: I don't like others because they threaten to take away what is mine, such as my sexual partner, my money, or my resources. My goal is to never be jealous. *List some examples of my being jealous, writing down the who and the why.*

3. Envy: With this cousin of jealousy, I resent others for having what I want. It is a feeling of discontent aroused by others' possessions, qualities, attributes, or luck. My goal is to always want the best for others. *List the people I envy and why.*

4. Doubt: Doubt is the biggest destroyer of dreams. My goal is to always practice persistence toward goals despite my doubts. *List doubts that I have, writing down the what and the why.*

5. Worrying: When I dwell on troubles over which I have no control, I become anxious. My goal is never to worry about things I have no control over. *List things I worry about which I have no control over.*

6. Revenge: This character defect involves righting a wrong with another wrong—"an eye for an eye"—when the actual solution is forgiveness. When I hurt others, I hurt myself. My goal is to forgive everyone, wishing them happiness, peace, and joy in this life. That, in turn, will set me free. *List those people I would like to seek revenge against, and why. (You may wish to review your Resentments List, above.)*

7. Sloth: This character defect involves the reluctance to work or to contribute to one's own expenses. If sloth is unrelated to physical or mental incapabilities, it is a form of selfishness. My goal is to always earn my own way. *List how I am slothful, and why.*

8. Gluttony: When I eat excessively, I hurt myself by becoming overweight and suffering from all the associated health problems. My goal is to take excellent care of my body and my health. *List examples of how I am gluttonous, and why.*

9. Lust: Strong sexual desire is not bad unless I harm others or myself, or am dishonest with others for sexual motives. My goal is for my sexual relations to be totally honest and cause harm to no one. *List examples of how my sexual desires have harmed others, and why. (You may wish to review your Intimate Relations List, above.)*

10. Controlling: Control involves imposing my will on others. My goal is to always live and let live. *List examples of how I try to control others, and why.*

11. Pride: Pride has two completely opposite definitions, one positive and one negative. The positive definition refers to feelings of self-worth and self-respect. The negative definition refers to feelings of vanity and arrogance, which are actually a mask for low self-esteem. Positive pride is associated with giving, whereas negative pride is associated with taking. My goal is to seek humility and to become more giving and of service to others, which leads me to positive pride and turns me away from negative pride. *List examples of how I display positive and negative pride, and why.*

Step 3: Reviewing All Four of Your Inventories with Your Mentor

Once you complete all four inventories in Step 2, arrange a meeting with your mentor to humbly and honestly go over all the lists together, being open to feedback that helps you to see things that you could not see on your own.

This step will take courage and humility to follow through on. It requires you to trust another person with intimate details about yourself, making you vulnerable to him or her. You may be apprehensive about doing this, but you will find that once you start to truly open up to another human being, it will feel like lifting a weight off your shoulders. By being truly honest about yourself with another person, you will find that your mentor will be able to help you to uncover more of your responsibility for your own resentments—which we called "My Part" in the resentments list you filled out above in Step 2.

You may think you did a good job of listing your part when you were completing that list, but I can tell you from experience that another person can help you to uncover and see more of your faults than you can on your own. The mentor's main job is to point out your own part in causing your resentments, so that you can change your future behavior by becoming accountable for how you have minimized or justified hurting others in the past. You need other people to help you see those things about yourself. Over time, you will become better at seeing your part on your own, but in the beginning, you are mostly blind to it without help from another. Again, accepting help from a mentor in this way will initially take courage and humility—but it will be the beginning of an incredible bond and friendship.

There is great value in someone knowing who you really are, with the insight to then give you valuable feedback. That will prepare you for the future, when you will mentor others. However, you must be a student before you can become a teacher. Receiving feedback from a mentor is not about being shamed for your bad behavior. Rather, it is about being open to reviewing your behavior, taking accountability for it, and not being a victim.

Reviewing all your inventories with a mentor will ignite powerful changes in your life, enabling a positive direction for your future. Once you start this process with another person who has a genuine loving intent to help you grow, you will want to share more with him or her, and to become increasingly open to getting feedback. It is a leap into practicing humility. By being willing to take this step, you will make real progress in your own growth, which will lead to a better life for yourself and everyone you know by allowing another person to help you remove the blocks that are in the way of you becoming an Expert Giver.

After completing your inventory lists and reviewing them entirely and honestly with your mentor, you should tell him or her any secrets that you feel shame or guilt about. Secrets eat at us from the inside and keep us sick. When they are shared with another person, that takes away most of their power. In turn, your mentor may share with you a secret that has weighed him or her down. If your secrets involve a crime for which you could be jailed, you can describe it in general terms so as not to reveal exact details, or you may choose to share the secrets anonymously with a priest.

This kind of trust makes for the strongest possible friendships and bonds, creating a cycle of giving and receiving. Helping you is helping me, and vice versa. In this process between you and your mentor, both of you give and receive. You are giving your mentor your trust and opportunities for him or her to give back to you. It is always a two-way street of healthy giving and receiving. Both parties benefit. It's a win-win situation.

You will experience all this from the other side when you become a mentor yourself. There will be no greater joy or reward for you than to become trusted by others, to be a part of their success and growth, and to create genuine bonds with them based on trust. In that relationship, your only intention will be to want the other person to grow, succeed, become less self-centered, and start helping and connecting with others. Nothing feels better than that.

Step 4: Making a List of Amends and Reviewing It with Your Mentor

Make a list of amends that you owe to others, and then review the list with your mentor.

First, go back to your Resentment List #3 (Your Part), and reexamine those resentments that you learned you had a part in creating. Those resentments will become the bulk of your Amends List.

Second, go back and review your Intimate Relationship List, adding those individuals to your list whom you think you owe an amends.

You do not have to review your Forgiveness List, because you have already practiced forgiveness with anyone on that list (e.g., the Male Mugger), and you do not have to make amends to anyone on that list, because you did not harm anyone on that list (they harmed you).

Fourth, think of people or organizations who are not on any of your previous lists, but you harmed in some way, such as by lying, stealing, or cheating. Add them to your Amends List, which is now complete.

Remember—and this is *very* important—you are not yet doing Step 5. That is, you are not yet making amends. And you are not yet deciding *if* and *how* you will make amends. You are only making a list of the amends you *may* need to make. If you have an urge to make some amends immediately, resist.

First, you need to meet with your mentor and review the amends that you wish to make and how you wish to make them. Then, with the mentor's feedback, determine which amends to make now, which ones to make later, and which ones not to make at all. You do not want to make any amends that will cause harm to anyone else in any way. Make all these decisions with your mentor.

Remember, you are accountable to your mentor, whose role is to help you become a better giver, and to prevent you from ignorantly harming others. If you make amends your way, without first consulting your mentor, you can do unnecessary harm. This is especially true if you make amends to former romantic partners, which can cause more harm than good. When you contact a former romantic partner to apologize, be certain that you do not have a sexual motive. Remember, amends are not about you feeling better while making someone else feel worse. It is for you and your mentor to decide together when making amends is needed.

Your mentor will also help you to decide the best way to make your amends. It may be face-to-face, over the phone, through e-mail, anonymously, or not at all. In some cases, not contacting the injured party *is* the amends you need to make. To confess to cheating on a former partner just to get it off your chest will only cause further harm. That is selfish and not recommended. If you are planning on confessing to cheating on a current partner, your amends may be *not* to tell him or her, but instead to resolve never to cheat on anyone ever again. This is called a "living amends."

Then there are financial amends, which may involve owing people or organizations money that you have borrowed or stolen. How do you make those wrongs right? Do you call up a person or company and admit a crime, thereby putting your freedom and income in jeopardy? No, especially if other people depend on your income. This falls under the category of amends that cause further harm.

In some cases, it may be best to come up with a plan with

your mentor to repay money anonymously. If you cannot find the people to repay, or they have died, you can repay them indirectly by donating to some cause they may have approved of. In some cases, it is best not to make the amends immediately, but to wait for the best timing. Your plan of action concerning your amends should be discussed and decided with your mentor.

Step 5: Making Your Amends

After you review with your mentor which amends to make and how to make them, start making those amends.

Now that you have gone over with your mentor which amends to make and which not to make, and the how and when to make them, you can begin to make them without delay. Some may require you to wait for an opportunity to present itself. With money that you owe, you should pay it back immediately, assuming you are able to. Otherwise, immediately start a payment plan with the individual or company, as you decided earlier with your mentor. Once you have worked out the specifics of each amends, including the methods and the timing, you can move forward with courage.

After the amends process begins, you will start to experience a freedom and peace that you had not previously known. You will have a new perspective on life. Self-pity will fade away. Your desire to help others will grow, and selfishness will begin to fade and be less of a challenge. You will become less interested in selfish things, and more interested in helping others. Your fear of people and economic insecurity will leave you. You will have new meaning and purpose in your life that you didn't have before. You will experience a level of happiness, joy, wisdom, and peace previously unknown to you.

Step 6: Take a Daily Personal Inventory and Promptly Admit When You Are Wrong

Every day, complete your Daily Personal Inventory (see below), reviewing your resentments, intimate relationships, fears, and character defects. Write down any new amends to review with your mentor, and practice forgiveness when the need arises. Also, evaluate your giving during the day, determining whether it was unconditional, or if you gave with conditional selfish motives.

Denial and instincts are powerful forces that never go away. So long as we are human, we are never fully cured of our instinctual drives, desires, and motives, which direct us to be selfish. That part of us will always take more and give less. It usually dominates our choices if we leave ourselves unaccountable and unchecked.

At the end of each day, take your personal inventory. I suggest either printing out several copies of the Daily Personal Inventory table provided below, or getting a notebook in which, while you refer to the table, you only write down any new items that come up. I also suggest that you have a weekly meeting with your mentor to go over your Daily Personal Inventory, in order to maintain accountability to yourself and another.

First, examine any new resentments you may have. If you need to make amends to anyone, list those to discuss with your mentor how and when you will make them. If you need to forgive anyone, start practicing the forgiveness as described in Step 2, above.

Second, review if you experienced any character defects today, thinking about how you can improve.

Third, examine if you were selfish, dishonest, inconsiderate, or jealous in your intimate relationship(s) today. And write down what you could have done differently.

Fourth, list any new fears you may have experienced that day, and write down whether they affected your financial, emotional, or personal security or your sexual relations.

Fifth, write down examples of how you gave to others throughout the day, noting in each case whether you gave unconditionally or with financial or sexual motives.

Taking a Daily Personal Inventory, meeting with your mentor to discuss your Daily Inventories weekly, and regularly attending Expert Giver Groups are all ongoing actions to maintain progress in becoming a more Expert Giver.

Table 6: Daily Personal Inventory

Resentment List #1 (Offenders)	*Resentment List #2 (What Happened / Instincts Affected)*	*Resentment List #3 (My Part)*	*Resentment List #4 (Forgiveness, when I have no part)*

Intimate Relationships Review
Selfishness:
Dishonesty:
Inconsideration:
Jealousy:
Alternative Behavior:

Character Defects
Greed:
Jealousy:
Envy:
Doubt:
Worrying:
Revenge:
Sloth:
Gluttony:
Lust:
Controlling:
Pride:

Fears

Amends

Was My Giving Unconditional or Conditional Today?

Step 7: Mentoring Others

Mentor others who are willing to go through the above steps. Be as unconditionally giving as you can in service to others. Be open to starting an Expert Giver Group in your area.

Now that you have completed the previous 6 steps, you can offer your guidance as a mentor to other people. You now have the experience to walk others through the steps.

When an Expert Giver Group is just beginning, the participants will not yet have experience completing the 7 Steps of Expert Giver Groups. Thus, at first, the participants will pair up to mentor each other. But as the group matures, newer members can decide whether or not to select their mentors from more experienced members.

When someone agrees to be your mentor, arrange a weekly time to get together with the goal of discussing and working through the 7 Steps.

For more information on finding an existing group or starting a new one, go to *www.ExpertGiver.com.*

The Ten Guidelines of Expert Giver Groups (Long Form)

1. *Our common welfare comes first. Personal development depends on the unity of the group.*

Unity is priority. Any personal ambitions or desires should not be allowed to affect or interfere with the group. And no individual has the authority to punish or expel any other member from the group.

2. *Leaders in Expert Giver Groups are trusted servants; they do not govern.*

When someone decides to start an Expert Giver Group, he or she initially assumes the three roles of Chairperson, Secretary, and Treasurer. When the group has three or more members, they can decide how to divide up these responsibilities.

The *Chairperson* leads the general meetings and business meetings.

The *Treasurer* takes money from a passed basket, banks it, pays rent and other bills with it, and makes a regular report at the group's monthly business meeting.

The *Secretary* takes notes at business meetings, keeps a list of members with contact information, and posts meeting notices on the web.

All of these positions are voluntary and temporary, with specific term limits to be decided at the first business meeting.

Initially, the Chairperson finds a location for the meetings, arranges terms for rent, if any, decides on a time to hold the weekly meetings, and posts the time and location on the web at *ExpertGiver.com.* The meetings can be held in a member's home or in a church or library.

When starting the very first general meeting, the Chairperson will propose a date and time for the monthly business meeting, to be agreed upon by the members. The date and time of the business meeting, which will be open to all members, will be announced at the beginning of every subsequent general meeting. At the first business meeting, and those following, the goal is to fill positions for the group with voluntary commitments from the members. The business meetings should operate according to Roberts Rules of Order (available at *ExpertGiver.com*), a simple formal way to hold meetings in an orderly fashion.

3. *The only requirement for membership in an Expert Giver Group is the desire to become an Expert Giver.*

You are a member of an Expert Giver Group if you say you are. No one may be refused.

There are no religious or political belief requirements, and no membership regulations of any kind.

4. *Each Expert Giver Group is autonomous.*

Autonomous means that every Expert Giver Group can manage its affairs exactly as its members please. An Expert Giver Group should never affiliate itself with anything or anyone else. With respect to its own affairs, each Expert Giver Group should be responsible to no other authority.

5. *The purpose of each Expert Giver Group is to support the methods and content provided by the 7 Steps.*

6. *An Expert Giver Group should never give or lend the Expert Giver Group name to any facility or outside enterprise.*

An Expert Giver Group should never go into business of any kind.

7. *Every Expert Giver Group should be fully self-supporting, declining outside contributions.*

Each Expert Giver Group should be fully supported by the voluntary contributions of its own members.

There is to be no public solicitation of funds using the name Expert Giver Groups.

The Treasurer of each Expert Giver Group should only collect and maintain a prudent reserve of money. It is up to each group to determine at its first business meeting, by a majority vote, what that prudent reserve level should be, as well as what its expenses should be. One suggestion for a prudent reserve would be to have enough money to cover the group's rent for two months. If the reserve ever exceeds that level, any further voluntary collections occurring at meetings should cease until funds return to a two-month prudent reserve level. Aside from rent, a group's expenses might include providing snacks and beverages at its meetings.

8. *Expert Giver Groups should remain forever voluntary and nonprofessional.*

The Trusted Servants and the mentors should never be paid for their services. In fact, members should never pay other members for any services related to the Seven Steps.

9. *Expert Giver Groups have no opinions on outside issues, so the name Expert Giver Groups should never be drawn into public controversy.*

Expert Giver Groups should never take a stance or side concerning any public controversy or argument. The sole purpose of the groups is outlined in the 7 Steps. All other advice or influence should be kept out of the meetings. Expert Giver Groups have no opinions on outside issues.

All information and opinions provided in the book Expert Giver by Jason Cazes, aside from "Chapter 20: Expert Giver Groups," are suggested topics of discussion at Expert Giver Group meetings. The meetings should primarily focus on the content of Chapter 20: Expert Giver Groups and the Seven Steps. I suggest keeping political and religious debates outside of meetings.

10. *At general meetings, there is to be no discussion of outside business of any nature. At business meetings, the discussion is to be confined to the group's business.*

The Ten Guidelines of Expert Giver Groups (Short Form)

1. *Our common welfare comes first. Personal development depends on the unity of the group.*

2. *Leaders in Expert Giver Groups are trusted servants; they do not govern.*

3. *The only requirement for membership in an Expert Giver Group is the desire to become an Expert Giver.*

4. *Each Expert Giver Group is autonomous.*

5. *The purpose of each Expert Giver Group is to support the methods and content provided by the 7 Steps.*

6. *An Expert Giver Group should never give or lend the Expert Giver Group name to any facility or outside enterprise.*

7. *Every Expert Giver Group should be fully self-supporting, declining outside contributions.*

8. *Expert Giver Groups should remain forever voluntary and nonprofessional.*

9. *Expert Giver Groups have no opinions on outside issues, so the name Expert Giver Groups should never be drawn into public controversy.*

10. *At general meetings, there is to be no discussion of outside business of any nature. At business meetings, the discussion is to be confined to the group's business.*

Suggested Guidelines for Opening and Closing Expert Giver Group Meetings

At the beginning of every meeting, I suggest that the Chairperson read aloud the Short Form of the Seven Steps, the Short Form of the Ten Guidelines, and then read the following:

Expert Giver Groups are fellowships of men and women who share their experiences, strengths, and hopes with each other with honesty, open-mindedness, humility, and a willingness to become less selfish, striving to live by the Golden Rule: *Do unto others as you would have others do unto you.*

There are no dues or fees for membership. Each Expert Giver Group is self-supporting through the contributions of its participants. The groups are not allied with any sect, denomination, religion, political party, organization, or institution. They do not wish to engage in public controversy, and neither endorse nor oppose any causes. Their primary purpose is for all the members to support each other in becoming Expert Givers.

This is a one-hour meeting from 7:00 to 8:00 P.M. (the length and time of the meeting may vary).

If you have a cellphone, please silence it.

Are there any newcomers attending their first, second, or third meeting? If so, please introduce yourself by your first name only, so that we may welcome you.

Everything said here in the group meeting and outside from member to member must be held in confidence.

At this time, we break briefly for the seventh guideline,

which states that "Every Expert Giver Group should be fully self-supporting, declining outside contributions." We have no dues or fees required. A basket is passed to cover the expense of rent.

(Pass the basket)

Are there any announcements for the good of Expert Giver Groups?

(Members make announcements)

Meeting discussion should adhere to the content of the Seven Steps of Expert Giver Groups.

Please keep your sharing to a time limit in consideration of the size of the meeting, allowing others a chance to share. (A timer, such as on a cellphone, may be used by a volunteer to assist with this.)

The topic for this meeting will be _____

_____.

(The Chairperson will briefly share with the group about the topic and then invite the members to share. Topics may include one of the Seven Steps)

At the closing of every meeting, I suggest that the Chairperson read the following statement:

I would like to say that the opinions expressed here were strictly those of the individuals who gave them. Take what you like and leave the rest.

The things you heard were spoken in confidence and should be treated as confidential. Keep them within the walls of these rooms.

Let there be no gossip or criticism of one another.
Please join me in closing…

(Stand up, hold hands, and then repeat the following together, line by line:)

> I will do my best
> in all circumstances
> to be kind, patient, tolerant,
> humble, unconditionally giving, and forgiving
> with everyone.
> So be it.

CPSIA information can be obtained
at www.ICGtesting.com
Printed in the USA
LVHW081313220520
656301LV00019B/1910